The Life-giving Path

Reflections for personal exploration and discovery

Helen Warwick

**kevin
mayhew**

kevin mayhew

First published in Great Britain in 2016 by Kevin Mayhew Ltd
Buxhall, Stowmarket, Suffolk IP14 3BW
Tel: +44 (0) 1449 737978 Fax: +44 (0) 1449 737834
E-mail: info@kevinmayhew.com

www.kevinmayhew.com

9 8 7 6 5 4 3 2 1 0

ISBN 978 1 84867 811 8
Catalogue No. 1501505

Cover design by Rob Mortonson
© Images used under licence from Shutterstock Inc.
Edited by Virginia Rounding
Typeset by Melody-Anne Lee

Printed and bound in Great Britain

Endorsements

This is a lovely book, beautifully written. Helen Warwick's spiritual wisdom and personal experience shine as we are guided through rooms and spaces of retreat house and garden, rich with metaphors, symbols and stories, ancient and modern. Theological, biological, and psychological gems are to be found everywhere, and they are thoroughly sound and helpful for making a soul-nurturing environment. It takes mindfulness to another level – becoming a responsible reflector and observer of life, with love for the world, for others, and vitally for self, one's many different selves. Creativity, playing and dreaming are developed as nourishments, and inspiring exercises and practical advice offer full care for mind and body, the home of spirit. One can savour almost every sentence as each page comes alive with divine and human love. This book belongs with the classics, to be read and re-read as a spiritually uplifting and immensely practical daily companion.

Dr David McDonald, Consultant Psychiatrist and Trustee to The Guild of Health and St Raphael

Reading *The Life-giving Path* allows you to visit a virtual retreat centre whenever you pick up its pages. Weaving thoughtful and wide-ranging reflections into her consideration of every room or space, from kitchen to chapel, and out into the garden, Helen Warwick encourages you to review all aspects of your humanity in a nurturing, creative, and prayerful context. The book is ingeniously structured with exercises to prompt your own responses, and even some deftly sketched retreat staff. There are also two fictional retreat-attenders, whose journeys you can follow at the end of every chapter, as you also explore your own. I highly recommend this well-written and helpful work as something to be read and re-read over the years.

> *Dr Sarah Law, Senior Lecturer in Creative Writing, London Metropolitan University and Published Poet*

This book on the spiritual journey by Helen Warwick, although simple, is very far from simplistic. There are echoes of St Teresa of Avila and the Interior Castle and the Spiritual Exercises of St Ignatius of Loyola. Knowledge of these spiritual writers and also of person-centred counselling has enabled Helen to share an accompanied journey of both spiritual and psychological enlightenment. By using the metaphor of a house or home, she reminds us of the reality of our bodies being the (temple) home of the Holy Spirit and the embodied presence of Christ. With the various spiritual exercises included, this book is ideal for individual or group discussion and activities. I recommend this as a suitable gift for those who are new to spiritual direction and wish to find a way in to this particular ministry.

Revd Stanley Baxter, Director of Mission, Holy Rood House, Centre for Health and Pastoral Care. Vice-Chair of Guild of Health and Spiritual Director

As I began to read this, I soon found myself very much hoping that I might be asked to edit it; but as I read chapter one I began to hope rather that it would be published but someone else would do the editing. That was because I was being powerfully affected by the chapter, and becoming aware of my own need for more reflective time – and in particular my need to read and use this book slowly and carefully.

That says much about the quality of this book – and must similarly speak of the personal qualities of its author. The latter insight adds value to the book as there is a feeling of being nurtured on a personal level – something very difficult for an author to achieve in print, but here it comes across effortlessly.

The author uses the image of a retreat house to create the feeling of being on retreat, and I think that many readers, like this one, will feel the need to take time in each 'room' – to read slowly and reflectively, and indeed to return from time to time to a room previously visited and read/reflect again. I am sure that I shall, as I continue to read, find my own favourite rooms to which I return more frequently, as well as somewhere I need to exercise more discipline in taking time there. This is indeed a valuable book if it inspires people in that way.

Revd Michael Forster, retired Senior Chaplin in a mental health and learning disability NHS Trust, Writer of hymns and books

For Emma, with much love

Contents

About the author

Helen Warwick is a writer and Spiritual Director. She leads creative courses and retreats and sees people on a one-to-one basis for spiritual accompaniment. She is a registered Occupational Therapist and has Counselling qualifications, including Person-Centred Art Therapy. She suffered a chronic illness for seven years, out of which developed many creative ways of finding healing and wholeness. Her own inner journey continues to be a creative and fulfilling one with God. Her hope is to work at a therapeutic retreat centre to expand the ideas in this book.

Acknowledgements

I am fortunate and blessed by many people in my life that help keep me connected to the path of life.

A special thanks to Nick whose loving presence is such an enabler in my writing. Anne and Jane – your regular phone calls are a continual strengthening support. Sue and Dave – thank you for our regular prayer times – yes, the book is actually finished! Dilys – thank you for your special presence and prayers.

A particular thanks to Jo, my spiritual director – your listening and creative input is so valuable to me. Anya, you have patiently given me regular treatments to help my flagging energy – your input and love is very much appreciated. Brian – thank you for supporting my vision. Your suggestion of writing it out led to the writing of this book. I value your voice in my life.

I appreciate my Worth supervision group for your support for my work in spiritual direction and for the fount of learning provided, some of which is included in this book. My PSG group provide an important creative space in my life – thank you.

My daughter Hannah was entrusted with version one of this book and I thank her for her encouraging comments.

Two other groups in the last two years have assisted my path of life – so thank you to the Quakers at Ifield and to my Monday Pilates group with Vicky.

I am grateful to all those I have worked with and thank you to those whose examples and stories appear in this book. I hope it will encourage us to realise that we all have a story and our stories can help each other just by their telling.

Emma, to whom this book is dedicated – you are often in my thoughts and, alongside many others I know who are in difficult circumstances, you give me much consideration on connecting to the path of life. I am thankful for your presence in my life and pray that this book may be an encouragement to your journey.

This book wouldn't be here without my publisher, so I thank the team at Kevin Mayhew for their work. A special thank you to Virginia, my editor, for her care and expertise in revising my manuscript.

I am eternally grateful for my relationship with God that informs and guides all of my life.

Introduction

Floating high above the Sussex countryside, perusing spacious houses with immaculate lawns and intricate flowerbeds, dipping down over a lake and rising again above the trees, was a wonderful experience giving me a unique perspective on life. This hot-air balloon ride with its gentle lulling motion and strange intimacy with others huddled in the basket gave me a perspective that I have only otherwise snatched briefly through the minuscule window of a plane. Viewing the scene from above showed me an outlook with a sense of wholeness; I was able to see how the river twisted and turned, embraced by a line of trees on each bank, and I could see the way the farm was organised, sharing the land with arable crops and fields for horses. The photos taken show a whole racetrack, the layout of a village and the way the roads cut through the land. The camera picked out hidden areas, only seen from the air – the small water holes surrounded by dense shrubs, the houses that have swimming pools and trampolines in their gardens. Down on the ground I could only experience these scenes as small pieces of the jigsaw; this trip gave me the opportunity to see the whole spread of this jigsaw, with all the pieces connected into this visual landscape.

This book offers the reader an opportunity to view their own life from a different perspective and get a sense of the whole. The different parts of our lives are examined through exploring various 'rooms' set in an imagined retreat house. The retreat starts in the personal room, giving ways to rise in our own hot-air balloon and observe our life.

This imagined retreat house is a large, comfortable place set in beautiful countryside. The word 'retreat' comes from the old French word 'retrere', meaning to draw back, and it is used to describe a place of seclusion. It is in this space that we will look at the various parts of our lives. The word can also be read as 're-treat', a chance to give precious time to oneself, something that is difficult to find in busy lives. My own experience of a retreat is a combination of thinking time, connecting to myself and having time to relax. I try and have regular retreats, from one-off days to staying over a few days. It is important for me to actually get out of my everyday environment, away from my usual routine and the responsibilities I carry and give myself time to just be me, without my attached roles. I can enjoy nature, hear the birds, breathe, move and free up my thoughts. I can connect creatively with my journey; writing and using colour for expression. It becomes a very freeing time, a time to listen to myself, to the sense of the divine in my life and sometimes to the input of others. In this reflective time I can re-assess my life, consider my hopes and my dreams and think about my connection to others. I can also consider my relationship with the sense of the 'more-than-myself', a divine presence in my life, one that I experience in many ways and learn about through my Bible and other resources. I always come back invigorated, refreshed and more at peace. This book will encourage a sense of retreat and observation of the different parts of life, allowing more understanding of what each of us is about and how we can connect to our dreams and purpose.

The ideas for this book are taken from my own journey through life that has included working as an occupational therapist and undertaking counselling training, including in person-centred art therapy. I now work as a spiritual director, running retreats and working individually with people, and it is this voice that will be leading you through the retreat. As a spiritual director I offer a sacred space for directees to explore their own lives – the whole of their lives, not just the spiritual – listening, reflecting and helping them to dig deeper around issues. I accompany people on their journey and, as we travel, we are attentive to any connection of God in and around that journey. My job includes helping people to find who they truly are, what they are being drawn to do, and to find meaning in their life. I often use creativity to help reveal these deeply personal offerings. My directees and the people who come on my retreats have been a great inspiration to this book, as well as having experienced many of the ideas shown in the rooms. My own creative journey and my faith have been observed in detail throughout a long chronic illness and continue to be noted in a life of much better health. I have done much study on finding a healthier way, including gaining insights into energy, nutrition and mental health, and I now use many therapeutic and psychological techniques to bring more fulfilment into my life and the lives of others. I have tried to avoid too much scientific or theological detail in order to keep the flow of the book.

The idea of a therapeutic, holistic retreat centre set in beautiful surroundings, with the chapel offering a centre of stillness and the other rooms providing practical and creative interventions, emotional and spiritual support and the all-important home-cooked food, derives from a passion of mine to see such work developed in reality.

As we travel through the different rooms of this retreat, noticing areas of our lives, there will be opportunities to observe which parts we struggle with, and how they could become more life-giving. One of the intriguing sights whilst floating high above the countryside was the outline of our hot-air balloon, appearing as a shadow on the ground. Whenever we had the sun behind us, we could see an imprint of the balloon many metres below. Some areas of life can feel as though they have a shadow cast over them, while others can seem to be facing in a more positive, sun-filled direction. I am very aware of the shadow and light in my own life. There can be parts of me that have different ratings on the satisfaction scale, but I am also aware that they can form different paths within me. I can easily get dragged down the shadow path through my thought processes and stirred emotions. It is a path that can be very subtle and enticing but affects my mood and energy levels, often leaving me demotivated. I am also aware of being drawn to another path, one of light, one that gives me energy, joy and a feeling of purpose. This life-giving path can be elusive, needing a different way of thinking and an awareness of the jigsaw pieces within me. It is a path that has led me to much wholeness and healing.

There can be tension within us between the shadow and the light in all stages of our lives. At a very young age my daughter gave some insight into the struggles with her paths. She would watch the lively boys at her playgroup and the mischief they created. Aged four, she announced, 'Sometimes I want to be a boy and sometimes I want to be a girl.' When I enquired what she felt like doing when she was a boy, she said, 'Something wicked, like throwing my toys or playing naughty mummies and daddies!' As a girl, she said she would play something good like good mummies and daddies. She always invited both 'naughty' and 'good' to her parties! There seemed more attraction for my daughter to what she knew to be 'wicked', as it looked so much more fun and inviting, but she was also aware of the pull towards other aspects of her life.

David, the shepherd boy turned king, wrote a song about his life-giving path that was connected to the God he had found. 'You show me the path of life. In your presence there is fullness of joy' (Psalm 16:11). Somehow David had connected to a God that was able to show him a path to travel that brought joy and blessings even through times of intense suffering. The God David describes is the same God who said to the Israelites: 'This day I call the heavens and the earth as witnesses against you that I have set before you life and death, blessings and curses. Now choose life, so that you and your children may live and that you may love the Lord your God, listen to his voice, and hold fast to him. For the Lord is your life' (Deuteronomy 30:19, 20). This God is very aware of the two different paths in our lives – one of life and blessings, and the other of death and curses. As we go through the retreat there will be practical and creative ways of exploring aspects of both these paths in our lives, noticing the shadows and light in different areas of our make-up and what might be blocking a connection to a more positive way of life. Alongside my own experience, there will be the stories and inspiration of others to draw us to a more life-giving way. The Appendix offers further exploration through creative exercises to enhance the experience of this retreat. The number of each exercise will be noted in the relevant part of the text.

There are staff who work at this retreat centre: the manager and those who run the house, cleaning, cooking and making it a comfortable, homely place. Jan is the chaplain; Karen is a trained listener, being trained as a spiritual director and counsellor; and Miles works in the creative space, with his training in art therapy. There are two guests already staying at the retreat, Vanessa and Mike, who will be sharing their experiences as they journey through the rooms.

Before you enter the retreat, you may like to plan to set aside some time so you can go through the rooms at a pace that is right for you to be able to take in what may be of benefit. Try and travel light; I would encourage you to take only yourself and a notebook and pen. Once you are ready, follow me, down the long drive and into the house.

Personal Room

Ways of reflection and observation

'Turn your eyes inward, look into your own depths, learn first to know yourself.'

Sigmund Freud[1]

The personal room is your own private en-suite room in the retreat with a comfy bed, desk and a lovely view. There is space here to relax and reflect.

Chris Hadfield's video of himself playing a version of David Bowie's 'Space Oddity' has been viewed online over 20 million times. What made this video so extraordinary was the fact that he was thousands of miles from the earth at the time, as an astronaut in the International Space Station. In an interview Chris stated that it is disorientating being in space and in the first few days of orbit most astronauts look for a familiar landmark on the earth, but after a few days the perspective lens widens and the whole world can be taken in. My trip in the hot-air balloon is paltry compared to a journey into space, but it also taught me something of perspective. There are

---

1. Quoted in *Events* (The Institute of Psycho-Analysis, Spring 1997).

ways to adjust our own perspective on life. Astronauts not only have to adjust to the wider perspective of seeing the textures and colours of the world and the infinity beyond, but they also need to re-adjust once back on earth. They can suffer many psychological problems, but one particular childhood event helped Chris to cope with this change in perspective. His teacher had taken his class to a deserted parking lot, given them each a piece of string and told them to mark off a square foot of ground and spend the hour studying it. Chris remembers clearly that if you took the time to notice, there was a fascinating amount of things happening in one square foot of earth. He could see the world of wonder that exists in this one square of ordinary nature and knew he could never be bored.[2]

This personal room is where we can try and see our lives from a different perspective, not examining every square foot of ourselves, but stepping back to observe different aspects of our lives, covered more fully in the various rooms, so we can notice more detail and get a sense of the whole. It was Socrates who said that the unexamined life is not worth living. When we start to take time to reflect on our lives we can begin to notice the everyday life that we lead, the events of our day and our responses to these events and happenings. Wisdom seems to come from experience that is reflected upon,

2. http://www.theguardian.com/science/2013/oct/26/chris-hadfield-astronaut-space-interview.

rather than from the experience itself, so taking time to sit and note the experiences can lead to an insight into who we are and how we work. We are all unique individuals, so noting how our mind works, what stirs our emotions, what our passions and gifts are, can all help piece together the person we are. It can also help to piece together the direction we are meant to be heading.

Finding the path that is life-giving for us has a lot to do with living a life that makes us feel fulfilled and gives us hope and meaning. If we are unaware of what our likes and dislikes are, what our inner desires are, what we hope for and dream about, then it will be harder to find this path.

As we note these resonances, we can start to find a hidden life within us – a life that is our real life, our actual experience, which is not in the everyday events that we do each day, but in our response to those happenings. It is a life within that we can connect to through being and listening to what is going on with our feelings and thoughts. This underlying life resonates at the centre of our being. For me there is a sacred space that I connect to where I listen and learn from the responses in my life, and this is connected to a sacred core within. There are so many different words for this core of our existence – the soul, the image of God within, or what the humanist tradition would call identity and integrity. I like the term Thomas Merton calls this centre, which is the true self. Finding out more about myself, my gifts and passions, what intrigues and catches my eye, will draw me to this centre, my true self, telling me who I am and bringing me nearer to my Creator and who I am created to be.

Terminology can be tricky when talking of the divine. The actual word 'God' can be a problem, as this word will conjure up many different thoughts and images for people. What I am meaning by the word 'God' is a presence that is outside of myself – a 'more-than-myself' presence – and yet also within me. This Creator God, with essence in all life, has this essence within each unique individual.

The Desert Fathers understood human beings to be part of the creation that God called good, special in that they are made in the image of God. Gregory of Nyssa spoke often of 'returning to the grace of that image which was established in you from the beginning'. Gregory saw it as our lifelong task to find out what part of the divine image God has chosen to reveal in us. Like the other early monks, he suggested that we can best do this by realistically determining how God has made us – what our primary faults and temptations are, as well as our gifts – not merely so that we might feel good about ourselves, but so that we might become an individual with more connection to God and share God's grace with others.[3]

3. See Kathleen Norris, *The Cloister Walk* (Penguin, 1997), p.143.

I find it an exciting thought that somehow by noting more about myself, I can reveal not only more of who I am, but also more of the image of God within me.

Coming into this personal room and entering into our inner space can be a difficult step to take. There will be much within that we may have to face and God is a one of mystery where we may be faced with surprises. The monastery where I occasionally go to spend a day in retreat has a welcome booklet for retreatants. It mentions that it is not unusual for the new visitor, having been shown around the monastery and to their own room, to have disappeared by the first meal-time. They have become too uncomfortable at the thought of the silence ahead of them; the time without the crutches of communication and the uneasiness of facing themselves and what God might want to reveal. Retreats provide a place of rest and refreshment, but also offer the retreatant an opportunity to find more of the path of life, which requires courage as well as discipline.

This God whose seed is in each one of us and also surrounds us is one that I have found highlighted, in many aspects of divinity, through so many sources: my own experience, the natural world, other people, the Bible and other books are just some of those sources. Jesus highlights many of the aspects of God, explored through his human form. He is an inspiration to the observer position. The mountainside was a place where he often went to pray and reflect. From here he could also observe – he was able to see the disciples in trouble on Lake Galilee, for instance, in the story mentioned later in this chapter. To explore this observer position and see what it was saying into my life, I used this story as a reflection with a small group I am part of, where we used our imaginations to sit on the mountainside with Jesus (see *Exercise 1*). Being able to imagine sitting in this position with Jesus and looking down at our present situation helped to bring a sense of overview on our lives. I was aware of the boggy ground below me and got a sense of the stepping stones that might appear to get me through that bog. Another member of the group could see a crashed vehicle down in the valley and felt it revealed to her that she had to review parts of her life. She was comforted by the calm lake the other side of the vehicle, where there was a coracle which seemed to be about future exploration.

It is difficult to find this underlying inner world, but observing our lives takes us on an exploration that helps us to connect to our inner lives. It also connects us to hearing the aspect of the divine. Many people struggle with how to hear God in their lives. There will be suggestions throughout the rooms of the retreat of ways to hear more of this voice of love, wisdom and encouragement. The exercise of reflecting from the mountainside fosters the ability to talk through what is seen with the imaginary presence of Jesus and then to listen to his perspective. This may feel very strange – talking to a spiritual presence

– but it can be very affirming, bringing thoughts and emotions that are meaningful to us out into the open. It can develop a way of listening to the perspective of the divine. This perspective can often surprise and offer us ways through life that can seem clearer and more life-giving.

As we reflect on our life we may note what draws us to a better way and the struggles we have that seem to drag us down a more difficult path. Scott Peck comments on these tensions within:

> . . . no matter how seemingly healthy and spiritually evolved we are, there is still a part of us, however small, that does not want to exert ourselves, that clings to the old and familiar, fearful of any change or effort, desiring comfort at any cost and absence of pain at any price, even if the penalty be ineffectiveness, stagnation or regression . . . the healthy self, however, must always be vigilant against the laziness of the sick self that still lurks within us. In this one respect human beings are all equal. Within each and every one of us there are two selves, one sick and one healthy – the life urge and the death urge.[4]

Peck notices the different pulls we have within, and highlights the importance of this noticing. It takes

---

4. M. Scott Peck, *The Road Less Travelled* (Rider, 1987), p.295.

inspiration to change from our old ways to one that is new and more energised, and as we travel through the rooms of the retreat we can become more aware of these struggles within ourselves.

St Ignatius, who founded the Jesuit order (or Society of Jesus) in the fifteenth century, was very aware of how reflection helped in understanding these two different paths of life. He recommended practising the 'Examen' (see *Exercise 2*), taking a short time each day to go through the day, noting what has resonated with us, what we have reacted to, what has made us smile and what we have found difficult. As we sit quietly, maybe aware of God's presence, we can become more aware of the two different paths that can be in our lives – one of light and life, the other of shadows and demotivation. Noting what has brought us joy, gratitude or peace, maybe an increase in energy, highlights what is drawing us to our path of life. Noting where there has been a drain in our energy, what has led to unrest or turmoil shows us what could be drawing us away from this path. St Ignatius expected that God would speak through our deepest feelings and yearnings, believing that our feelings are a reflection of what God is doing. This is an important aspect of the Examen. Emotions are hard to pinpoint and name. We are often unsure of what we are feeling. Taking time to be aware of our feelings can help us to note these important messengers and what they might be saying about our situation. They highlight what we react to, and this can help us explore different areas in our lives. This exercise is a useful one to develop throughout this retreat, noticing your reaction to what you read. I will be bringing a wide spectrum of thoughts, some of which will resonate with you, others of which may jar. Noting your reactions to what is offered in each room will be useful for your own journey, helping you decide which ideas to take on board and which to leave behind.

I have found that, whether sitting quietly reflecting on the happenings of the day or taking an overview of my life from the aspect of the mountainside, it is the observer position that has transformed my life. It is a technique I have also used in a closer context to make a connection to my body and its different aspects. It is like viewing myself through a video camera. It is difficult working out how we operate – what goes on in our heads and what emotions we are feeling. In the observer position we can notice our thoughts and what ticks over in our minds and how we react as we go through our day. As our skills of awareness increase, we may be able to note any emotions that are around for us and maybe even feel where they are in the body. In the quiet of the personal room we can note what tensions may be in the body, where the pains and distress of the everyday are being held.

When I started observing my mind I noticed my thoughts were all over the place. They were like an untrained pet dog, leading me down unpleasant alleyways and into corners where I felt stuck. I watched the effect these thoughts had on my body and emotions. The more I observed the more confident I felt to start training this 'dog'. I could note which thoughts were dragging me down a path that I felt was unhelpful to me. I could start to change the pattern of my thoughts, stopping them from going down alleyways that looked a bit dark and uninviting, seeing the areas where they were getting stuck and letting my dog rest at regular intervals so he didn't get wound up and too jumpy. This also helped me to appreciate my mind and what it actually did mull over. These reflections will be continued when we visit the library.

Ben Watt wrote an excellent book on his personal story of a life-threatening illness where he spent two and a half months in hospital. He learnt to appreciate listening to and observing his internal thoughts. At one point a visitor brings him a pile of books: 'He thought I must be bored witless, not knowing – how could he? – that the middle distance and the inside of my own head were more interesting than books.' He summarises:

> Hospital taught me a new language with a different rhythm that goes on inside our heads all the time, a ceaseless stream and current of thoughts and words, babbling and pulling through all our waking hours. I learnt to listen to it, like listening to the sea from a bedroom window. At first you don't hear it, and then you realize that it

is underpinning every sound, and it has its own rhythms and pulse. And it took me elsewhere, shell-less, into myself, where meaning came from loneliness and calmness, acceptance, adaptability, gratitude and making peace with oneself.[5]

Ben found through having this time when he was truly alone he got to hear what was going on internally. He discovered meaning from what he found – a path through his suffering. We are often oblivious to many of our own thoughts, and finding a way of revealing them can be really enlightening. Now as I do a mundane job, such as housework, I can note what is going on in my head, just observing what is popping up for me. I can choose whether I want to continue those thoughts (what sort of response are they drawing from me?) or switch them off and think about something else. The effect is very liberating.

Reflecting brings to consciousness memories to mull over, emotions to feel and experiences to talk about. Thoughts that are very jumbled and chaotic may be observed, and these may need the space of the listening room (where there are trained listeners) to be worked through. This helps to ground them and allows them to be integrated into a better state within. Psychotherapist Fiona Gardner encourages us to develop our thinking.

---

5. Ben Watt, *Patient - the true story of a rare illness* (Bloomsbury, 2014), p.110.

When talking about using reflection to observe our memories, she notes:

> This capacity to think through what has happened to us in the past, and how it affects us in the present, is a long and hard-won process. This is not about self-indulgent self-absorption or introspective navel-gazing. It is about fully developing the ability to mentally represent feeling states and sensations, and analysing and integrating them in a way that allows us to let go of the past, and live in the present free from fear of the future.[6]

The way of the observer is not to become more self-centred, but to be able to note aspects of ourselves that will lead to a better way – not only for us, but also for those with whom we live and interact.

I have found that as I reflect on my daily happenings I get to understand myself more; what I like and dislike, what attracts me and what annoys. I also enjoy noticing images brought up that I would have missed about my day if I had not taken some time out. I might remember the robin that was enjoying snacking on the bird table, or the pleasure I felt from watching some children playing. I have got to know what interests me and how wide-ranging that is – from lichen to patterns. I can see how this reflection also helps others as I encourage my directees to notice and reflect and see them becoming

---

6. Fiona Gardner, *Journeying Home* (Darton, Longman & Todd, 2004), p.84.

more confident in knowing and being themselves. Gradually we are finding out about the true person God has made us to be. Finding ways of getting to know ourselves assists with our decision-making, identifying our purpose in life and discovering a richness that connects specifically to our own individual journey.

The detached stance of the observer can also have tremendous health benefits. Being able to look at thoughts that are anxious, fearful or depressed, for example, from outside these emotions can help us to see them more clearly and learn their message and where they may have stemmed from. Viktor Frankl was a prisoner in Auschwitz for three years. Throughout this terrible suffering he found that forcing his thoughts onto another subject was helpful. He saw himself in a lecture room giving a lecture on the psychology of the camp. Both he and his troubles became the object of an interesting study. He observed his sufferings as if they were already of the past; this included his emotions which ceased to be suffering as soon as a clear picture was formed of what they were about. So he was able to rise above the situation and he went on to develop a form of psychotherapy he called 'logotherapy', based on the methods he used to survive.[7]

Once, when I was ill, I was looking at the Bible story in Mark 6 in which Jesus sends the disciples into a boat while he goes to pray. A storm blows up on the lake and the disciples start to frantically try and save themselves.

7. See Viktor E. Frankl, *Man's Search for Meaning* (Random House, 1955).

Jesus notices what is happening and goes out to them, walking on the water, but they do not recognise him and are frightened. He has to reassure them and climb into the boat. I had a picture of myself in a boat. I had the choice of either keeping my focus on myself and the boat itself – for example, by fretting about my situation – or of looking beyond the boat to what might be happening. The observer position was a good one to use from inside the boat from which I could look out and see around myself, connecting to a bigger picture where there might be reasons for my illness and a destination in view. This position meant that I could be detached from immediate desires that might be getting in the way of the right path at that time. The disciples were frantically focused on themselves within the boat, an understandable reaction to chaos. Had they adopted the observer position and looked beyond the boat, they might have recognised Jesus and been reassured by his presence.

This part of the retreat sets up important skills to help find the path of life. Being an observer and hence a reflector on our own lives means that we are taking responsibility for our own development, finding what questions are around for us, what our desires are and noting what our path is like at present. Coming into this personal room for reflection also reinforces that we matter. Each of us is unique, a wonderfully made individual who can contribute in our own special way to society. Taking personal notes as you go through the retreat will help you to bring together your own story, and identify and reinforce your skills and passions. 'What lies before us and what lies behind us are small matters compared to what lies within us. And when we bring what is within out into the world, miracles happen.'[8]

For Consideration

- What are my feelings about exploring my own personal space?
- What do I want to get out of this retreat?
- What do I notice when I start observing my life?

Vanessa's Story

Vanessa was nervous as she entered the retreat. She had never been away on one before and did not know what to expect. She was not sure how she would fill her time and knew they had no television or radio for distraction. Her home was always a hectic environment, with her husband and two teenage girls, but she wanted to get away to review her life. She was aware of a general feeling of anxiety that she couldn't shift, and she wasn't sleeping well at night. Thoughts kept crowding in as she tried to resolve some of the issues affecting her. She wasn't sure whether stopping her everyday life would help her anxiety or whether it

---

8. Henry David Thoreau, http://www.betterworld.net/heroes/pages-t/thoreau-quotes.htm.

might get more intense as reality started to hit home. However, she knew that she had to take this risk of seeing what God might want to draw her to or say to her; to give God a chance to voice something, and herself a chance to hear it. Besides, she had heard good things about this place and it was lovely to get all her meals provided.

Vanessa had brought with her a small book called *Sleeping with Bread*.[9] This encouraged a daily practice of reflecting on life, noticing each day what had happened that she could be grateful for, and also noticing what had been difficult. She thought that would be a good start for her. She would sit with her notebook and jot down what she noticed about her life at present – what she liked and what made her uncomfortable.

Mike's Story

Mike settled himself into the retreat house. He had been before but it was a long time ago with an old friend. This time he was on his own. He was going through a rough time in his life; he had just been made redundant, due to poor health. He wasn't really sure who he was without his work; he felt very lost and not sure what to do with himself.

Mike was unsure how to start his reflections but decided to write down some facts about his situation. Being away from home helped him to see himself a bit

---

9. D. Linn, S. Fabricant Linn and M. Linn, *Sleeping with Bread* (Paulist Press, 1995).

more clearly. He saw himself in his mind's eye going through what he did and how he carried out his life. He saw a man becoming older than he needed to be, a reluctant man, very lost with many feelings around that he didn't understand. He didn't really like the picture he saw and was relieved that there were staff in the retreat who might be able to help him.

The Chapel

Finding life through connection with the divine and exploring the inner spirit

'God comes to us disguised as our life.'

Richard Rohr[10]

> The chapel is a beautiful room with a huge window at one end looking out over the garden. A carved wooden altar adorned with a small wooden cross is placed in front of this window. It is a room where there is space to reflect and pray.

Mary Fisher was a determined missionary of the seventeenth century. She had felt called in her Quaker silences to visit the Sultan of Turkey as part of her journeying to the Ottoman Empire. She set off in 1657; the boat journey ran into difficulties and she ended up having to walk more than five hundred miles to the Sultan's palace in Adrianople. No one knows how she managed this walk and it was not until 1658 that she reached the palace. Here no one would take her into

---

10. Richard Rohr, *The Art of Looking Sideways* (CD from talks at Greenbelt 2010) – http://www.greenbelt.org.uk/media/talks/contributor:richard-rohr/.

the presence of the Sultan as he was a formidable man, always with an executioner at hand. Eventually she succeeded in gaining an interview with the Grand Vizier, a man of great age and cunning. Mary was not afraid, having encountered much cruelty in her life, and the Grand Vizier was taken with this woman who showed no fear. He arranged for her to have an interview with the Sultan the next day. The Sultan received Mary Fisher as an ambassador; she had said that she was bringing him a message from God. Surrounded by his court officials in their magnificent costumes, the young man sat, decked out in a cloth of gold. Mary advanced and stood before him, wearing her simple Quaker dress. She stood there and waited in silent prayer to hear the words she needed to say as she had brought no prepared message. Then at last she began to speak, appealing to that of God in the hearts of her hearers. The Turks listened gravely and attentively until she and the interpreter had finished.

'Is that the whole of the message?' asked the Sultan. 'Yes,' replied Mary. 'Hast thou understood?' 'Every word,' said the Sultan. 'And it was the Truth.'[11]

It is not just the courage of Mary Fisher but also her way of hearing the voice of God that I find inspiring in this story. The Quakers believe that God is within each person and they use silence to still themselves to

11. See Elfrida Vipont, *The Story of Quakerism 1652-1952* (Bannisdale Press, 1954).

become more aware of the spirit within and its guiding voice. Mary was able to stay in the present moment, not getting anxious or intimidated, but standing with faith and certainty, knowing of God's enabling. It astounds me that during her walk of more than five hundred miles she had not gone over and over a speech, which I certainly would have done had I been meeting a despot!

In a survey carried out in 2009 it was found that 70 per cent of people in the UK believed in a human soul, 55 per cent believed in heaven and 53 per cent believed in life after death.[12] There are many people who recognise a divine centre and a spiritual realm and, as we come into the chapel, there will be an opportunity to explore our own connection to the God within and to consider how this connects us to the life-giving path. Our bodies need air, food and water to stay alive, but we also need to consider the connection to our human spirit, this 'essential life-force that motivates and vitalizes human existence'.[13] It is this spirit that connects mind and body and is linked with our emotions. Connecting to the path of life needs a recognition of our human spirit within, this dynamic life-force that motivates us to discover purpose, hope and a relationship with something outside of ourselves. Our spirituality is the way that we respond to our spirit.

---

12. See http://news.bbc.co.uk/1/hi/uk/7996187.stm.
13. John Swinton, *Spirituality and Mental Health Care: Rediscovering a 'Forgotten' Dimension* (Jessica Kingsley Publishers, 2001), p.14.

Keeping spiritually healthy includes using the skills of reflection and observation from the personal room to look at making sense of life situations and to find meaning in our lives. It involves noting how we connect to ourselves and to others, as well as looking at how we might connect to a power outside of ourselves, what we might term 'God'.[14]

These are big areas to think through and the chapel is a focal part of this retreat for us to explore our spiritual health. There can be many diverse ways of discovering God; we are all unique, so there will be different connections to the life source for each individual. Sister Wendy Beckett believes that people are in contact with God when they are looking at beauty. She sees God in all art, from ballet to pictures of hunting scenes. Thomas Keating, a Trappist monk, points out that religion is only one way to come to God. Nature, spiritual friendship, conjugal love, service of others and art are just a few of the ways that God calls us to this path of life. Keating likens the paths to the spokes of a wheel where God is in the centre: all paths lead to this divine centre which is also their source. As we travel towards the centre, we come closer to the other paths to strengthen our unity with God. For example, someone who has taken the religious path may begin to perceive the wonders of God in nature as a further means of uniting with God.[15]

14. Ibid., p.25.
15. Thomas Keating, *The Better Part: Stages of Contemplative Living* (Continuum, 2007), p.106.

I like this image with its suggestion that, as we travel to the centre of this wheel, not only do we become closer to other paths of life, but are also more united with different aspects of God as well as with other people on their life paths.

This illustration may also challenge the images we hold of God. As we travel through the rooms of this retreat house, we need to find the God who will help our individual path, and draw us towards becoming more whole and healed. An image of God that is restrictive – maybe a God who is watching our every move and wants to punish us – will keep us from the life that God is really offering. Often, as our life changes, we may find ourselves outgrowing the image we have of God. Our lives may get bigger, but if the God we found in our early life is not challenged, it may remain as an image that is not helpful. Finding what gives us life, what we are drawn to, that which excites, energises, brings love, hope, beauty and creativity will all be drawing us to God at the source in the wheel's centre. We can have a connection to this source of life within us. The symbol of the wheel can develop into our own personal wheel as the spokes connect to an inner divine source at the centre of our being. The external circumference of the wheel connects to the external divine source, thus bringing many opportunities to link the God of our outside experience with the inner spirit.

There are various ways we can explore the divine. In the chapel there are short services that take place regularly – services where people can come to worship, hear the Bible, to share in communion and to pray. Communal services give an opportunity to allow our thoughts to be guided through worship and prayer, rather than trying to run life our own way. They can provide a rhythm to help connect our lives to this 'more-than-ourselves' other. (There are numerous resources now available to assist our regular worship. I like the *Celtic Daily Prayer* with its richness of inspirational prayers, readings and stories from the Northumbria Community.[16]) Sharing the Eucharist can be a reminder of the life-giving presence of God and be a sacred act that unites us to others. Singing worshipful hymns, choruses and chants can add other aspects to our prayer, often connecting to our emotions. St Augustine said that he who sings prays twice. Listening to the chaplain's insights into the Bible and doing our own reading can help us explore this God who draws us to a more light-filled path. There are many books and study guides to aid our reflections.

The first book of the Bible, Genesis, tells how God created life at the beginning of the world. The earth was a formless, empty, dark, chaotic place. The first thing that God created was light to avert the chaos. This was an energy which formed 'day', which in

---

16. The Northumbria Community, *Celtic Daily Prayer* (Collins, 2005); seehttp://www.northumbriacommunity.org/offices/how-to-use-daily-office/.

Hebrew signifies warmth and heat. This was separated from the darkness, so right from the formation of the world there is a distinct separation between light and dark, symbolising two aspects of life. Both have their importance. In the Gospel of John, Christ is introduced as Creator, the Word who was with God and was God. 'All that came to be was alive with his life, and that life was the light of men' (John 1:4, New English Bible). The following verse speaks of this light that can never be extinguished or be mastered by the darkness. It is this light that we can connect to within to overcome the tensions we experience with the darkness.

Ian Mobsby, an Anglican priest, uses the attributes of God as Creator, Redeemer and Sustainer as a gender-neutral alternative to 'Father, Son and Holy Spirit'. He explains that the Eastern Church has a concept of the Trinity as a dynamic dance, leading at different stages in history.

> The very nature of God is centred on creativity, love and intimacy; a creativity that led to the pouring out of a divine love that created the whole cosmos. All matter, both animate and inanimate, was therefore created out of the expression of love internally generated within the Trinity, and expressed out into the infinity of space and time.

So the whole of creation has come out of the inner worship and creativity of God.[17]

Creation involves spontaneity, joy and beauty, and this captures the life that God offers us.

This path of life is described as one that continues from our human form on the earth to a life after our human body has deceased.[18] The eternal life that God offers has a timelessness, and is something that we can tap into now. The moments when we lose track of time, when life flows, when we are doing something that we are passionate about, can be glimpses of this timelessness. There can be a sense of being drawn to a more perfect world within the noticings of our earthly world; the vibrations of joy and beauty, love and hope, draw us to the eternal life offered by God.

We can read and learn about aspects of God but we also need some sort of experience of this presence to be drawn to this path of life. In the personal room there was mention of having a conversation with the divine. One of the aspects of prayer is developing a personal conversation where we are able to voice our concerns, emotions, and events in our lives to a 'more-than-ourselves' other and then try and listen to what this other might be inputting into our journey. It is difficult to listen without first finding a way to still the body and mind, and the chapel can be a good place to sit in silence and try out ways to

---

17. Ian Mobsby, *God Unknown* (Canterbury Press, 2012), p.27.
18. See, for example, John 5:24 and 2 Corinthians 5:1.

stillness. There are various techniques that may be helpful in finding a way to calm the mind and still the body so that we can travel to an inner space where we can listen to ourselves and God (see *Exercise 3*). Whatever method is tried, it is useful to start with just a few minutes and then build up to 20 or 30 minutes. The mind is very good at telling us that this is all a waste of time and we should be doing something much more useful. The mind always needs something to fix upon and it is often when I try to be silent that my thoughts start to chatter. However, if I can still my thoughts, using these various techniques, then gradually I come into my still centre. Focusing on breathing, for instance, can really help the mind to calm and come into the present moment, where we are aware of what our senses are noting. Going through what we can hear, feel, smell and see, can help to keep us in that present moment, stopping our minds ticking over other things. If thoughts do pop into our heads – which they will – then trying just to let them go, maybe imagining them like clouds drifting over us, can be a help.

There have been many studies into the health benefits of meditation or ways of calming the mind, suggesting that we are less anxious and sleep better and that the creative parts of our brain are opened up when we meditate. Added to this, finding a way to still our mind and body prepares us to be receptive to the source of life within us, to the light that can dispel darkness. 'Be still, and know that I am God!' (Psalm 46:10) is a lovely verse that describes what can happen through the stillness. There is something about inactivity, about just allowing ourselves to be, what I name as a 'here I am, Lord' position, that is a very humble gesture that can bring about a knowing of this sacred inner space. Although it is a 'simply being' state, there is an opening of the internal eyes and ears so there is an expectancy of connecting with the divine, to which our human spirit is drawn. I find this state of active listening helpful; sitting in awareness of, but not absorbed by, what is going on in my body, in my thoughts and my surroundings. This awareness is an alertness that is just noting where I am and what is going on; just listening to any promptings of the inner spirit. The noises that I hear around me are the outer skin of the silence within.

Stilling ourselves can lead to a contemplative state where we are not thinking about anything in particular, and are not focused on any one feeling, idea or object, but are merely wide open to God and Mystery. It is a state that can centre us as we are often distracted, divided, and chaotic within. It can re-collect our attention and make us feel more whole and at peace, as the fragmented parts of ourselves are connected to our centre. The practice of contemplation takes us to a deep wordless place where there will be fleeting glimpses of the life-giving path, tastes of peace, joy and love as well as sometimes unsettling things. Stopping all activity can allow difficult thoughts and inner turmoil to surface. It is important just to observe what surfaces and not get caught up in the emotions that might arise. It is worth noting that it is often when we are pulled into a darker, more difficult place that the path of life is revealed. Isaiah 45:3 says: 'I will give you the treasures of darkness and riches hidden in secret places, so that you may know that it is I, the Lord, the God of Israel, who call you by your name.' Sometimes a word or image may come to mind, a memory or thought that can be like a glimmer of treasure in the darkness. The more the stillness is practised, the more a sense of the divine can be recognised within. It might be a noticing of emotions, a sense of peace, an awareness of an inner wisdom, a greater strength or energy experienced. This can affect our everyday life. We may start to make changes, we may think and act differently, be challenged over what we are doing, review our relationships. If the changes draw us more to aspects of God such as love, beauty and peace, then we will know that in these times of stillness something is happening.

It can be through sitting quietly, making a still space within and opening our inner ears and eyes, that we start to become open to the path to our inner divine, this human soul or true self. It is a way that can be hard to keep open. I had a picture of a hazelnut where the kernel is the seed, the essence of this inner way, and the shell is my hard exterior, needing to be penetrated so that I can find this precious kernel. It is the kernel that is linked to the experience of aliveness, connecting to the indwelling divine. As Jesus said, 'the kingdom of God is within you' (Luke 17:21). Finding stillness connects me to this kernel through making the hard shell more porous. It is so easy to shut off from God and live my life from the hard exterior only. It is often when I am tired, or feel unsafe, wanting clear boundaries or feeling lost, that I connect to what seems like a protective hard shell, therefore losing contact with the kernel.

C.G. Jung had some interesting theories that link to this kernel picture. He noted that the first half of one's life is spent building up the ego-self. The ego is formed as a protective shell, needed as an important structure for identity, and could be represented by the shell in my illustration. It refers to the 'I' part of us, the part that forms our wants and desires. Having built the strong shell, there needs to be a time of sorting the interior, connecting to the Self inside the shell. Jung referred to the Self as our deepest reality, in which the ego-self is grounded, and he called the process of transformation, of connecting with the Self, 'individuation'.[19] For me, working out how to keep a path to my kernel, to the essence of myself or to my true self as I would name Jung's Self, means working with the perspective and an awareness of the divine. The path of life and blessings that God mentioned to the Israelites in Deuteronomy 30 is the path connecting to

---

19. See Frieda Fordham, *An Introduction to Jung's Psychology* (Penguin, 1991).

the true self, whilst the path of curses and death is a life without connection to our interior, to our inner wisdom and to God; we are not really living, just going through the mechanisms of survival.

Allowing a path to the kernel means a letting go or refocusing from the shell, the hard exterior. The shell has built up over the years and can be a protection for our souls, but it can also get in the way if we do not learn to make it porous. I was exploring this concept during a retreat one year. It was a time when my health was not good and I was anxious about attending a forthcoming conference as I did not know how my energy would be. I realised that I needed to not close down under my hard shell through the illness, but be open as to how God might be guiding me. I felt that if I did not do these things that seemed right for me to do, then I would not have the opportunity to bring in outside influence to allow the kernel to grow and blossom. St Paul showed that he had been able to integrate his hard shell: 'My ego is no longer central. It is no longer important that I appear righteous before you or have your good opinion, and I am no longer driven to impress God. Christ lives in me' (Galatians 2:20, *The Message*). John Sanford comments on this passage:

> In this statement Paul tells us that his personality has been re-organised in such a way that it no longer revolves around his Ego, but around a

larger centre within himself that he calls Christ within. This is the essential thought – that in the course of our lifetime our personalities are to be transformed and re-organised in such a way that the Ego, with its ambitions and goals, is no longer the main reference point.[20]

Finding our path will gradually get clearer as we connect to more life-giving ways. The more the ego shell is cracked and we make tracks to our inner core, the more light will be shed on the way to travel (see *Exercise 4*). I try to set aside regular times to allow an opening to my core. As well as sitting and becoming still, I find being in nature, walking and gardening, creating with art and stitching, and finding a regular rhythm in swimming, all help me to find states where I am attentive and listening. Jesus was able to be open to God's power throughout his ministry and took himself away when he needed to replenish his daily needs. He was able to keep the path open to his kernel with his life-line to God that sustained all that he did. I like this sense of what prayer is all about – not a striving or asking, an active spiritual doing, but allowing ways to open up the path to our kernel and keep a link to God and that essence in creation.

Opening up this path means that we can receive from God. The things that sustain us, such as love, come as

20. Quoted in Sue Monk Kidd, *When the Heart Waits* (HarperOne, 2006), p.54.

gifts, only if we are open to them. I was once reflecting on these thoughts while I was on holiday, looking out over some lovely scenery with wild flowers, and some beautiful goldfinches flying about. I knew that I could just note this scene and leave it there, or I could go further and let it seep into my kernel, to allow myself to be porous and open and let the beauty touch me. Somehow I knew that this would unlock the joy and creativity of the Spirit within, so that I could know a sense of God's presence through this scene. Giving time to be open allows us to receive something of the care and love of God and the excitement of life itself.

For Consideration

- How do I find a connection with the divine and how does the divine connect to me?
- What ways could I use to find stillness?

Mike's Story

Mike had not had much time to explore his relationship with God when working. He knew he believed in God but questioned what this meant. The retreat was his way of trying to re-establish some sort of connection and see whether it would help with his direction in life. The first time he went into the chapel he got a real sense of calm.

It felt like when he had been caught in a heavy downpour and then stepped into the shelter of his home. The chapel was offering two short services a day, including a Bible reading, a short talk by the chaplain, Jan, some worship and sharing the Eucharist. He had a talk with Jan about how the services didn't seem as appealing as just sitting in the chapel in its enveloping silence. She encouraged him to do this, to just sit in God's presence and listen to what came up in his reflections. He appreciated the space to just sit with this great change going on in his life and to still his thoughts.

Vanessa's Story

Vanessa found herself a bit weepy in the services in the chapel and wasn't sure why, as she saw herself as quite a strong person. She felt something of the worship had touched her and this had made her feel rather vulnerable. It was all linked to stopping her regular activities. Usually she was too busy to spend time sitting and reflecting on her life. It was all somewhat overwhelming. There was something about the chapel that made it feel like just herself and God, and she wasn't sure she wanted to get too close. There was a lovely Taizé song that was sometimes played – 'O Lord, hear my prayer'. It was such an easy tune and was asking God to answer her when she called. She found the song going round in her head, so used it as her prayer for her retreat.

The Kitchen

The heart of the home; a place to explore physical and spiritual needs

'The primary business I must attend to every day is to fellowship with the Lord. The first concern is not how much I might serve the Lord, but how my inner man might be nourished.'

George Müller [21]

The kitchen is a spacious room, filled with equipment to cater for those on retreat. It has a side room offering a cosy place to make hot drinks and to sit at a table to reflect.

Martin Luther King spent hours honing his speech that was to be given to 250,000 civil rights activists gathered in Washington in August 1963. His team advised him not to use the line 'I have a dream' as it had already been used in other speeches. He was placed quite late in the line-up that day, after other speakers, songs and prayers. It was a hot day and, as he read from his script, he could tell that the crowd were getting restless and wanting to leave.

---

21. George Müller, *The Autobiography of George Müller* (Whitaker House, 1984), p.88.

He heard a voice behind him, prompting him to 'Tell 'em about your dream, Martin' – it was a good friend, one of the gospel singers on the stage. She had been moved in his previous speeches when he spoke of his dream. Eventually he put his notes aside and told the crowd what was on his heart. The rest is history and people all over the world are still responding to his speech.[22]

Once Martin Luther King started speaking from the heart he gave a more powerful message. He had to put down his own agenda first which freed him up to speak about his hopes and dreams. In the kitchen, often referred to as the heart of the home, we look at our connection to our hopes and dreams and where they could be leading us. The heart is an analogy for a precious area within, where hopes and dreams are created and where we store what is valuable to our journey. It is a sacred area that holds our true self and is connected to the source of our life. A heart set on the right focus is needed to take the body on the journey that is of light. A cluttered heart is one where the focus is lost, there is a lack of purpose and our needs and desires are unclear. This can make the kitchen a chaotic place, where food and drink may be used as comfort and to meet unfulfilled needs, rather than to sustain a healthy body. We will explore this room as a place of life for heart and body, trying to find the focus that is needed for the path of life.

22. See *The Week* (Dennis Publishing Ltd, 24 August 2013).

The eating disorders charity, Beat, carried out a survey of 857 respondents about emotional overeating. Eighty-eight per cent of those surveyed said they overate for emotional reasons, such as feeling low, anxious or lonely, because they couldn't cope with difficult feelings.[23] There will be more about difficult emotions when we get to the store cupboard, but here in the kitchen it is worth noting how our emotions have a big influence and how we often try to avoid their impact. The ways of reflection in the personal room help us to connect to our emotions, noting what stirs and excites us and what gives us pain and makes us uncomfortable. This can help us to clarify our feelings so we can start to identify their roots and begin to uncover our underlying needs. We all have our sensitive areas when it comes to our needs. One of my areas I have explored is not feeling understood. When this happens I used to withdraw and often turn to food for comfort. I had to note my reactions and reflect on my behaviour and look at other options that were more caring towards my body. This process helped me to highlight my need to be understood, so that I could be more prepared for times when it didn't happen.

As we learn to use the skills of reflection in the personal room, we start to open up a way to connect inwards and find out more about ourselves. The day-to-day requirements of life can get in the way of our

---

23. See http://www.b-eat.co.uk/assets/000/000/383/Beat_EOSG_survey_re-sults_original.pdf?1427212028.

connecting to our dreams. Busyness and ways we have to distract ourselves can draw us away from connecting to our true hopes and desires. Whilst our body and flesh deteriorate as we get older, the heart is a storage place that develops and enlarges as we link to our life-giving path. The experiences we go through and our emotional challenges, once reflected upon, can make it an enlarged place. I am reminded of a story of a person whose father died. Though her grief was ongoing, she was able to notice that this pain was enlarging her heart. She felt more compassion for others through this expansion.

I have also noted that doing things where I feel in my element enlarges my heart. When I connect to my life-giving path and have the right focus, then an image that comes to mind is of air being blown into a balloon, creating the right shape for that balloon. When I have challenges that I am able to reflect on and work through it feels as though my heart is accommodating new areas and expanding its shape: the shape that is right for my unique being. Similarly I can use this symbolism to reflect on when I feel the balloon becoming shrivelled, when my heart is being pulled out of shape, when I feel myself drifting onto a path that is not right for me. All sorts of distractions can affect my hopes – distractions such as my own doubts about myself, people who challenge what I am doing, and my fears over what I feel God may be asking of me. I know it is a matter of getting my priorities right, looking at the bigger purposes of my life – linking to the God of hope that will help me grow into the full shape I am destined to be.

We all have needs to which our desires and dreams will be attached. Our needs are very different from our wants. I connect my wants to my ego – the hard outer shell – whereas I connect my needs to the kernel, to what my true self is wanting. Recently I did an exercise that is often used by life-coaches called the *Wheel of Life*. On this wheel 12 areas were marked – work, health, leisure, self-esteem, focus, creativity, love-life, personal and spiritual growth, family, finance, relationships and home. The idea was to give each section a mark between 0 and 10 as to how satisfied you were with that area of your life. As each section was intersected on this scale, you could see how unbalanced your wheel was and which areas might need some attention. I could see this was a useful exercise but I nevertheless found myself getting very frustrated, and I realised that this was because I was being asked about satisfaction in these areas which seemed to connect me to my ego. There was a lot that niggled and this reminded me of my wants: all the things that would be great to make my life easier. When I connected this wheel to having God at the centre of the hub where all these areas joined, the exercise changed. I could see how I might need to give more attention to some areas, but I could also see how some that had lower marks, such as health might be enabling me to have a better connection to God (maybe more reliance and trust) and hence a more fulfilled and balanced life.

When I consider my needs, rather than my wants, I find quite a list, including: 'to be loved and wanted, to be part of a community, to be listened to, to gain insight and to pass insights on to others, to add to society in some way, to create, to reflect and keep a sense of momentum in my life'. These needs, which will differ for each person, will be underlying our desires and hopes. Our past will also influence our current desires, alongside our present circumstances. There will be more exploration of this in the listening room, but the kitchen is a good place in which to distinguish our needs from our wants and to recognise how they influence our dreams and desires. We may also need some prompts to note our unique desires. We can ask ourselves questions such as: 'What would I really want to happen in my life?'; 'If I could go anywhere or do anything, what would I do?'; and 'Where is God drawing me, or what do I feel encouraged to pursue?'

Our dreams and desires will be connected not only to our needs but also to the direction we are heading in life. Jeremiah 31:21 says: 'Set up road signs; put up guide posts. Take note of the highway, the road that you take.' This verse is a challenge to review where we are heading and what sort of road we are on. There can be many signs in our lives pointing down various routes. I was struck by an illustration in the film *War Horse* of the way one person had a particular focus for getting through life.

This person, a grandfather, cares for his granddaughter, not admitting to her that her parents have been killed in the war. The granddaughter becomes aware of her parents' death through another source and challenges her carer, accusing him of not being brave enough to tell her, but he uses the image of a homing pigeon to explain his decision. Homing pigeons were used to carry messages during the war because of their ability to head straight for home. They had to fly over the field of war, from one point to another; they were not to look down, but to focus only on getting home. The grandfather felt that if he had told his granddaughter all that had happened to her parents, she would have looked down – while his focus was on getting them through the war in the best way he could find. The homing pigeon has the skill of always being able to navigate towards home and it is worth asking ourselves what our hearts might be set on and in what direction we are navigating. We all have our own ways of getting through life and it can be hard to find the route that is life-giving but, as we get glimpses of this route throughout this retreat, it is worth noting a sign to keep us pointing in that direction. Such signs will point to what motivates and draws us. The guide posts in the verse from Jeremiah remind me of the right support needed as we travel, including people with whom we can share and from whom we can receive encouragement, and the right space in which to explore.

As we connect to our heart we can start to align ourselves to the true self that God intends us to be. For each of us there will be a God-given reason as to why we are made as we are and how our gifts can be used to achieve what is right for us. When we reflect on ourselves as children, we will notice that there were books we liked, perhaps symbols or characters that meant a lot to us, activities we enjoyed, and we have memories of when we were in our element. Children are very natural in showing their true selves if they are in a nurturing environment. They show their identity through their play, questions and interests. In our present time we can note what stories catch our eye in the newspaper or through people's retelling. As we explore, we will notice more of what excites and energises us, when we feel fulfilled and passionate about something and also what pulls us out of shape. This will all be adding to finding our true selves and our purpose in life. There are two exercises in the Appendix (*Exercises 5a* and *5b*) to explore the heart. We need to be heading where our passions are leading and where we find fulfilment in life. Martin Luther King had such a powerful impact as he was able to speak from this deep place of his hopes and dreams that were aligned with the purpose he was being led by God to fulfil. Becoming more ourselves will mean we bring our uniqueness into the world to add to it in some way.

It may be interesting to note at this stage how strong or weak our desire is to connect to faith and to the divine. I have had people say to me that they don't feel any connection to God, but that they do sense a desire for such a connection. St Gregory said: 'He who with his whole soul desires God, certainly already possesses the One he loves . . . The greater desire becomes, the more the soul rests in God. Possession increases in the same proportion as desire.'[24] The desire to explore God and the life-giving path, in whatever way, is more important than being able to feel or hear a spiritual sense. The more we desire to connect to a better way, the more of God we will find and the more our heart will find its right shape.

George Müller, who gave us the opening quote for the kitchen, was a missionary who was very clear about his purpose and kept his eyes focused on God. In the 1830s he embarked on an extraordinary mission to help orphaned children in Britain, although his main aim was to demonstrate the reality of God. He was disturbed by the faithlessness of his contemporaries and longed to have something to point to as visible proof that God was the same faithful God as always. So he focused on God, asking for what he needed in his prayers. People started to come to him with contributions and offers – from nurses, to people giving equipment, food and money. He encouraged people to ask God for what they needed, if they felt it was God's will, and then to persist

---

24. Quoted in Maureen Conroy, *The Discerning Heart: Discovering a Personal God* (Loyola University Press, 1993), p.71.

in prayer until this was resolved. He advocated having a great expectation of God. So through prayer, without ever asking anyone for money, without setting up any committees and without being paid a wage, he managed to set up five big orphanages (which helped over 9000 children), various schools and many other societies.

George tried not to get distracted from his focus. In his prayer-time he found that sitting still tended to encourage distractions, so every morning he walked, carrying his Bible, to meditate and talk with God. This may seem a daunting example to follow, but it is worth noting what drives us and produces the impetus that gets us through the day. George was drawn to the suffering of children and had the skills to administer these orphanages. We can notice what draws us and connects us to God to find how that might lead us in life.

Following the right signs for the path of life will encourage our body and help meet its needs. There will be more focus on the body in the next room, but the kitchen is especially linked to what sustains the body, not only spiritually but also with the food and drink we require. Having a hard look at our bodies, preferably by standing naked in front of a mirror, can help us assess what impact food is having on our bodies and may also offer indications of our state of health. Being overweight or underweight, having poor skin condition, lank hair or shadows under the eyes, for example, can all be pointers to how our bodies are reacting to our lifestyle and what we eat and drink.

In addition to observing our body, it is also worth noting our energy and mood. Excess food or drink will have an effect somewhere; we may become more sluggish, low in mood and demotivated. Some foods cause sensitivities in the body or take much energy to digest. Changes in energy or mood after eating, such as the heart speeding up or the mood becoming low, can be signs that what we have eaten is not the best for our bodies. It may be worth getting expert advice if we think certain foods may be causing us problems. We all have our own rhythm and metabolism so need to work out what our body requires, which may be very different from the requirements of the people who share our meal-times.

One key to life in the human body is its enzymes. These are chemical compounds that turn the food we eat into fuel for every single cell of the body. Within these cells, enzymes turn the fuel into usable energy, which makes our heart beat, our nerves fire and all other bodily functions take place. Nearly all enzymes in the body, of which there are thousands, depend directly or indirectly on the presence of vitamins and minerals. So to help these enzymes function at their peak, we need to give our bodies the right amount of nutrients.

Making changes to our diet can be difficult as food is a very social part of life and is tied up with our mood and emotions. Problems have sometimes existed since childhood when neglect or deprivation may have led to poor food habits, or when food may have been used as a punishment or reward. Eating behaviours become habits that are hard to break – for example, associating eating snacks with watching television. Using food as a reward or to temporarily reduce stress will associate food with a lift in mood, which means it will more likely become a habit – and habits can only be changed if they are noted. *Exercise 6* in the Appendix helps with observation of our food and drink. Individual requirements, lifestyle and environment need to be reflected upon, and the various seasons in our lives taken into account, when making changes. Making very gradual changes can be effective – changes that do not increase stress, as that may lead to wanting more comfort food! Increasing the intake of more healthy foods and eating less of those that are not helpful can be part of this gradual process. It also helps to think of other ways to reward or comfort ourselves, than through food or drink. What ways are there of encouraging ourselves that don't cost money?

Looking to sustain a healthy body will need a motive that is outside of ourselves. Isaiah writes of God's invitation: 'Why spend money on what is not bread, and your labour on what does not satisfy? Listen, listen to me and eat what is good, and you will delight in the richest of fare' (Isaiah 55:2). Trusting that God is able to offer a better source of comfort than food, or a better reward than we are offering our bodies, will point the signs in a divine direction. Times of temptation and frustration when food, drink or other stimulants seem the only option can lead us to connect more to ourselves as we try and find other ways of sitting with our discomfort. It can be a testing time trying to listen to God's ways, but it may help us find an alternative perspective on our needs.

Does connecting to a more fulfilling path involve accepting that food and drink are part of God's gifts for us, and learning not to abuse that gift? If we look at what the natural world offers – all the trees and plants, animals and insects that we can eat – then we can appreciate that creation offers an abundance of food that gives us the right nutrition. Nuts, grains, vegetables, fruits, legumes, meats, fish, honey and oils all come from these naturally created God-given foods. We are now faced with an array of food that does not fit this category; much is processed, has many added chemicals and would be unrecognisable to our forebears.

In my search for better health, I found that there are many foods that tend to sap energy and cause problems with health. The following list highlights some of these foods and suggests better alternatives:

- Sugar messes up the body's metabolic rate and insulin production. It disrupts the balance of essential minerals and weakens the immune system. Better alternatives are molasses, maple syrup, xylitol and honey.

- Preservatives and additives compromise the immune system and can be carcinogenic.

- Processed meats are preserved with nitrites (which can convert during cooking to nitrosamines, which are carcinogenic) and are high in salt and saturated fats.

- Salt retains water and increases blood pressure.

- Refined foods such as white sugar, cakes, biscuits, white bread and white rice have had the goodness stripped out of them and contain empty calories. Better alternatives are whole grains, oatcakes, brown rice and wholemeal bread and pasta.

- Stimulants such as coffee, tea and alcohol deplete vitamins and minerals in the body. Coffee and tea also have a dehydrating effect. Better alternatives are barley cup, rooibos (redbush) tea, mate tea and herb and fruit teas.

- Dairy and wheat products are common allergens. They both contain large proteins that are hard to digest and can affect energy levels.[25]

---

25. The Institute of Optimum Nutrition is a good source of further information: http://www.ion.ac.uk/. The NHS and the Department of Health also have information on the web regarding different diets and healthy eating:http://www.nhs.uk/Livewell/loseweight/Pages/Loseweight-home.aspx and http://wwwdh.gov.uk/health/category/policy-areas/public-health/obesity-healthy-living/.

Having had a lot of problems with my energy levels over the last few years, I have done much research into the best way of feeding myself to allow for optimum energy levels, as well as helping the brain with fatigue symptoms. Something I find easy is sprouting my own food which increases the energy and nutrition provided by the food. Many seeds, beans and lentils can be sprouted, making this a cheap and useful way to ensure daily fresh-grown food. The dried products that I find work well to sprout are mung and aduki beans, green and brown lentils, and seeds such as alfalfa, broccoli, sunflower, cress and radish. After soaking for a few hours they can be sprouted cheaply on damp kitchen paper in a jam jar or, more effectively, in special seed sprouters. They need to be rinsed with water twice a day and will be ready in two to five days, bringing enjoyable taste, colour and health benefits to meals. Proteins such as meat, fish, eggs, lentils, beans, nuts and seeds are good for energy and essential for making neurotransmitters, which are vital for the thinking process. Some proteins contain the full amount of amino acids needed in the body while others are incomplete but, if eaten with other incomplete proteins, make up a complete protein, providing the full amount of amino acids. Sources of incomplete proteins are grains, nuts, beans, seeds and vegetables. By combining two or more of these, more amino acids become available to the body. So having beans on toast, lentils with rice or sprinkling seeds on our porridge will increase the nutritional value considerably. This can be especially helpful to vegetarians as complete proteins often come through animal sources.

To keep blood sugar levels steady it helps to eat at regular intervals, having three meals a day. Complex carbohydrates, such as whole grains, including brown rice, oats, corn and rye, are digested more slowly and so help to balance blood sugar; they also help to increase levels of serotonin, which is known for its mood-calming effect. People suffering from depression can benefit from eating regular complex carbohydrates. When blood sugar is low the body often craves foods that release energy quickly, such as sugary and refined foods. These give only an initial boost to energy and then lead to a bigger dip, often resulting in a lower mood than before the food was eaten.

The brain weighs only 2–3 per cent of our body weight but uses up around 25 per cent of our energy. It needs our care and, since it is about two-thirds fat, eating polyunsaturated fats found in olive oil, nuts, seeds, oily fish and avocados can help its function as well as help to maintain a balanced diet. Good fats also include omega-3, -6 and -9 fatty acids, which play a pivotal role in forming and maintaining the brain, central nervous system and all cell membranes. Supplements have helped alleviate many conditions from developmental problems in children, mental health problems, heart issues, inflammation, chronic fatigue and Alzheimer's.[26] Drinking water keeps the brain hydrated and helps the kidneys to eliminate waste products. Ninety-nine per cent of the chemical reactions in the body depend on water. Eight glasses a day are recommended (preferably between meals) or enough to keep the urine straw-coloured and not too dark.

It may seem surprising to combine in one chapter the heart as the wellspring of life with the best diet to feed our bodies, but there is something about this kitchen place, this place of reflecting, hearing the rhythm of our own heart, listening to its yearnings and emotions, that allows us to explore the needs of both our body and our spirit. I have had directees who, in exploring the heart, have found their body naturally wanting to follow a better way. They discover they go off certain foods and want to eat more healthily. There is a knowing in this place, an inner knowing that is beyond the grasp of the ordinary workings of the intellect. This is the centre where there is a possibility of living from a different place: one that is free from stress and anxiety, and where we can learn a different way of being.

---

26. See http://igennus.com/ for more information on omega fatty acids

For Consideration

- What are my dreams, hopes and desires?

- Where might they be leading me?

- What do I offer my body in food and drink? Does this connect to my appetite and sustain me? Does this draw my body to the path of life?

Mike's Story

Mike appreciated having some regular meals in the retreat. Though he could cook a decent meal, he wasn't good at being consistent with his eating. He found, being on his own, he wasn't very motivated in looking after himself. He booked some sessions with one of the staff members, Karen, in the retreat. He wanted to look at his needs, not just his physical needs but also others that had become pressing now that he was at a very different stage in his life. He didn't really know what he wanted to do in life; there was just this air of lostness around for him at present. Karen listened to his story, his current situation, and how he came to be in this place. She let him talk and helped him to summarise his main concerns. In another session Karen suggested they look at his gifts, what he felt he was good at, and how that would fit into his purpose in life. Mike had always liked woodwork, but had never followed this hobby through. Karen suggested he reflect on what he would like to be doing in ten years' time. If he was looking back from then, how would he like to see his life? She suggested he also did this exercise with the perspective of the divine; to sit with God over these thoughts and see what came up for him.

Vanessa's Story

Vanessa felt more confronted with aspects of her life in this retreat. At home, whenever she felt challenged or uncomfortable she squashed the feelings down. If she did get space to herself, feelings would often arise that made her restless and frankly rather alarmed. The biscuit tin offered a useful way of assuaging these feelings, and she got irritated with a friend who couldn't see why she bought biscuits if she was getting worried over her increasing pounds. She felt it was much better attacking the biscuits than taking her feelings out on the others in her house or on the crockery! Here in the retreat there was no biscuit tin and she knew she needed to sit with her frustrations and note what they were about. Her list of dislikes and likes was a good starting point for this consideration and she tried to think through various elements of her life. She knew she needed to earn money, run a house, keep up with relationships, connect with God and do her bit for society. However, this stopping in the retreat made her realise that, alongside her frustrations, she didn't really know why she was doing what she did; life was just trundling along.

Karen had suggested that she draw a large circle on a big sheet of paper to represent her heart. She was then to use colours and words to see what came up for her as she reflected on her heart, and to do this fairly swiftly without thinking too hard. She enjoyed using the colours and found symbols and words appearing in the space. 'Heaviness', 'hope' and 'blocked' were words that appeared, alongside some black that had yellow fracturing it like a lightning bolt. She sat with this heart and imagined it being held in God's hands. This gave her a feeling of peace and support.

The Spacious Room

Exploring the body and its connection to the life-giving path

'Understand the body not as a dumbbell that we are sentenced to carry for life, not as a beast of burden who carries us around for life, but as a series of doors and dreams and poems through which we can learn and know all manner of things.'

Clarissa Pinkola Estés [27]

> This is a room with no furniture, its four walls making a large square space, devoid of clutter. It is a light, airy room and there is a full-length mirror on one of the walls. The floor, with its smooth wood makes it easy for movement. This room is where the body can make itself heard.

During the most restricted times of my chronic illness I used to take myself off in my imagination and give my body space to move freely: to run, climb hills, splash in rivers and dance. I also visited a building that seemed to

---

27. Clarissa Pinkola Estés, *Women Who Run with the Wolves* (Rider, 1998), p.206.

connect to various needs in me. One of the rooms in this building was a dance studio – a plain, large room with a barre on the wall. Here I would stretch and move, while looking down over the garden at the back of the building. It seemed a healing process to allow my body to do the things it wanted to do, and was not able to do in reality. The movements I was able to do in my imagination became important in my healing and developed into the stretches and yoga I started to do in reality, and into the 'dance' moves in my lounge through which I expressed my emotions. The body taught me many things and was a great lead in drawing me to the path of life.

The body is a truly amazing organism. Each human body has more cells in it than there are stars in the universe. The outer skin is effectively replaced every month, while most of the body is renewed over a seven-year period. The immune system replaces its entire army every week and, when under viral attack, has the capacity to produce 200,000 new immune cells every second. Even the health of the gastrointestinal tract is maintained by about 300 different strains of bacteria and other micro-organisms; these are unique to each person, like the fingerprint. The digestive system produces 10 litres of digestive juices daily to break down the food we eat, roughly 100 tons in a lifetime. This is taken through our 'inner skin', the gastrointestinal wall, which effectively replaces itself every four days. All this unseen activity of the body is powered from only a small amount of food which also heats us and allows physical activity.[28] Yet despite the importance of our bodies, we are not really taught how best to look after them and to listen to our bodily needs. We often take notice only when our body is underperforming and not following our expectations. This spacious room allows exploration in understanding and listening to our bodies, and seeing how the body can be part of the connection to the path of life.

The Bible places great emphasis on the body. There are many rules in Leviticus, concerning hygiene, sex, handling food and coping with disease, which were heard as God's word and were very relevant to the Israelites at the time they were compiled. In the Psalms David expressed his delight to God at being so intricately made: 'My frame was not hidden from you when I was made in the secret place, when I was woven together in the depths of the earth. Your eyes saw my unformed body; all the days ordained for me were written in your book before one of them came to be' (Psalm 139:15-16). He states his whole body longs for God, suggesting a very physical link to God.[29] Jesus is the ultimate representation of the importance that God places on the body. He came in the flesh, in a body, and illustrates how our human body can be connected to God.

---

28. See http://www.ion.ac.uk/information/onarchives/wonderfulworld.
29. Psalm 63:1.

The last chapter suggested that we look at ourselves in a mirror to assess the body. I wonder what your thoughts are when you see your body in full – naked? Are you able to look at it and what are your feelings about this body? We tend to be very critical when we look at our bodies: our size and shape, lumps and bumps, appearance and imbalances all adding to the critique. The body can give us a hard time, so we may have resentment and annoyance at being lumbered with such a body, or frustration with the way we look. The body with all its demands is often seen as a burden, something that requires too much time to look after properly, so that it is left to fend for itself. Looking in the mirror can help us to really see what it is that we carry around and to connect to this body with which we have been blessed.

In order to feel integrated we need a balance between our body, mind, emotions and spirit. Usually we run our lives using the mind with its logic and rationality, allowing it to race ahead while the other areas are left unheard and neglected. Reasons are looked for when the body is not working as it should, doctors are consulted, the web is accessed. What is not taken into account is that each individual can have a way of understanding the needs of their own body: to hear what it requires and then to work out a way of fulfilling those requirements. Recent research has shown that the mind and the body are interlinked; the neurotransmitters, the chemicals that transmit impulses along the nerves have been found not only in the brain, but also being produced by internal organs. Thus not only can the brain produce thoughts that reach to every cell in the body, but also these messages can be initiated and transmitted by our organs too. Dr Candace Pert, of the National Institute of Mental Health, refers to the 'bodymind' – the mind and body working as an integrated whole, because at the level of the neurotransmitter there is no separation between the mind and the body.[30] The more we can connect to the body, the more it can help us with its messages.

Noticing and observing the body can be the start of this understanding. The body has its own in-built rhythms: its breathing rhythm, its daily and monthly cycle (men as well as women), and its heartbeat rhythm. Noting and listening to our own personal rhythms – how fast our heart beats at different times, how often we breathe, and how our energies are at different parts of the day and month – can connect us to our body and help our wellbeing. We all have our own body clock that sets the rhythm for the most effective functions of the body in the day and prepares the body for sleep at night. Many aspects can affect our rhythms: stress, shift work, ill health and getting older all have an impact on our sleep and waking patterns. Health is dependent on the rhythmic changes of these in-built cycles imposing order on the body, thereby enforcing stability through change.

---

30. See C. Pert, *Molecules of Emotion: The Scientific Basis Behind Mind-Body Medicine* (Scribner, 1997).

The earth has its various seasons and cycles and these can also affect our own body rhythms. It is well documented how a full moon can affect us psychologically with its gravitational pull and how different we can be in the winter than in the summer. So all these aspects need to be listened to and taken into account with our own individual bodies.

Focusing on the breath can be a helpful start to connecting to our bodies and hearing its rhythm. This requires stillness and time just to let our breath connect us to our body. For the most harmonious rhythm the in-breath needs to be the same length as the out-breath. Noticing this rhythm can also reveal whether the breathing is as effective as it could be, which is something that will affect our energy. Many people overuse their neck muscles when breathing, not using their diaphragm. This can cause tension around the neck which can affect the blood supply to the head and the circulation of the cerebrospinal fluid, causing fatigue. Breathing deeply into our lungs, not moving the shoulders, and allowing the breath to go down into the diaphragm can enable a more life-giving path. Many medical conditions stem from an imbalance between oxygen being breathed in and carbon dioxide being breathed out, so focusing on the breath and breathing exercises can help retrain the body to breathe in a more life-giving way. Singing can improve breathing, getting the oxygen circulated, as well as connecting to the emotions. In the Bible, singing is connected with new life; it is often a response from the people after God has responded to them. It is a good way of expressing ourselves and need not involve any particular tune. Allowing the body to make sounds and noises that it wants to express, especially on our out-breath, can feel as though we are connecting to deeper places within.

The biblical version of creation states that life comes from the breath of God, when God breathed into the nostrils of Adam after forming him from the dust. Another name for God's Spirit is *Ruach*, meaning breath or wind. God's breath, the spirit in us, brings us life. Jesus used his breath to breathe onto the disciples when he wanted them to receive God's Spirit. I know that my breath is very much linked to my physical wellbeing, as well as being a powerful source of energy of God's Spirit within. I use my imagination with my breathing to breathe into tensions or pockets of fear, knowing that it links to that life-giving Spirit.

St Paul talks about the body as being the temple of God's Spirit.[31] The temple had a central role in Jewish society; as well as the worship centre it was also the art gallery, concert plaza and poetry library. The temple symbolised the dwelling place of God. It was a place of communication with and about God, and its priests had access to the mind of God and instructed the people in the law. The building was also a potent symbol of

31. 1 Corinthians 6:19.

the life-giving ways of God. Comparing the body to the temple where God dwells would have been a very powerful symbol to those who heard this. They would have understood that Paul was describing the body as a sacred covering, as a place where God's centrality would influence the challenges of the body – such as sickness, disease and negative thoughts. It may have made them think of the body as the place where spirituality and creativity combined, where there is access for each individual to be in touch with the mind of God.

The temple was representative of God's entire creation: a microcosm of heaven and earth; a place that connects the spiritual and the worldly. Jesus was a living example of this temple symbol, referring to his body as a temple.[32] As the temple represented God's presence on earth, Jesus was naming himself as the fullness of that presence in bodily form. He connected heaven with earth, linking to the external and internal God. Paul was recognising that our own bodies contain this representation. 'For in Christ all the fullness of the Deity lives in bodily form, and you have been given fullness in Christ' (Colossians 2:9-10). I wonder how our perception of our body might change if we saw it as a vessel carrying the fullness of the Deity along with the effects of this fullness?

Using the senses is a key way of being more aware of our bodies, awakening us to them and helping us to 'learn

---

32. John 2:19-21.

all manner of things', as the opening quote suggests. Sitting in stillness and using our senses to become aware of what is going on in our body gets us in touch with different aspects of it. We could imagine what we might see if we looked at our body, using the observer position and noting the body from the outside, but also from the inside. What are we seeing through the lens of that imaginary camera? We can also listen to our bodies – to our heartbeat, to the inner noises of our body. What are these sounds telling us? Noting the tensions, pains and general feelings of our body requires an attention to the daily happenings. It is much easier to tell when things are changing in the body when there has been a relationship established with the body.

Heeding the non-verbal communication of the body helps with this relationship. The sinking feeling in the gut, when we sigh or fidget, when we grit our teeth and have tight fists – all these signs point to messages the body is revealing. It is telling us what we are reacting to, what is making an impact on us at the time. Acknowledging the impact on the body of what happens to us in everyday life can be an enlightening way to a greater understanding of ourselves. A person may be under the illusion that the path they are on is working out well, whereas the body may be giving away all sorts of signs that things are not going well at all. There may be tensions, stomach churnings, rapid blinking, and nightmares: many ways the body is trying to get its message across that somewhere along this path there are stumbling blocks. By listening to these signs we can start to trace back to when they began to appear.

By acknowledging and listening to the body's responses we have a chance to change, to turn around what is happening. I used to have a churning stomach that reacted frequently to fearful thoughts. Once I was aware of this, I was able to communicate with my stomach, to have a conversation with it and work out why it churned away. I consciously tried to relax that area, to let it flop! It helped me see the effect of the thoughts that created this reaction and to change these thoughts to something more positive. Communicating with the body may sound strange, but it is yet another way of strengthening the relationship. Asking the body what it needs and listening to the answer may bring surprising messages. Pinpointing certain areas of the body that are giving trouble and creatively working with these areas by having a conversation with that area or using paper to see what comes up in colour and shape when thinking of the problem, for example, can help us to understand what the body may be telling us. It might link into past events, bringing back memories that can be worked through, or it might highlight thinking processes that can be changed (see *Exercise* 7). It amazes me how the thoughts that pop into my head can actually cause a physical reaction in my body; I can notice a tightening around my neck muscles or a clenching of the teeth, for example. Some of the symptoms the body displays are psychosomatic – tensions and pains forming from stored emotions and painful memories. Using the senses and creative ways can help us to connect to other reasons for the body not functioning as well as it might, ways that only we can access.

The body has its own way of containing and expressing emotions. When I work with people and they are talking about an emotion – anxiety or fear, for example – then I sometimes get them to explain where they can feel that emotion in their body. It might be butterflies in the gut, tension in the neck or a pain in the head. I may also get them to explore it further – has it a shape or a colour? By working with the emotion and the body, it can become clearer what is happening, so allowing there to be something to work with. For example, if I explore my fear I may describe it as a great black blob in my stomach. I can then work with this black blob, rather than with something that I cannot really articulate. I can draw it out, or imagine it draining away, I can breathe into it the life of God, and as I breathe out I can imagine it leaving my body. I may also talk to God about it and see what this divine voice is saying to me. By using creative ways there will be much more understanding.

Using the senses not only helps us to understand and make a relationship with our bodies, it also allows the body to make a richer sense of the present moment as what we are hearing, seeing, touching, smelling and tasting connects us to the here and now. If I go out for a walk, I may be wrapped up in my own thoughts and be totally oblivious to what is going on around me. But if I am open to my senses while I walk and note the beautiful blossom on the tree, the lovely birdsong, the rough texture of the bark on the tree trunk, the scent of some flowers, I am connected to what is happening around me at that moment. It is in the present moment that God's presence can be most strongly felt, where a divineness can be recognised and heard. Connecting to our senses helps us to appreciate the present, what is going on for us in the here and now.

Mindfulness is a technique that is currently very popular, because it is having so many beneficial effects for people. It is a state of being alert to even the smallest and most ordinary details of life. It is a way of staying in the present moment through the senses and brings many benefits, such as calming and focusing the mind. Going through the day noticing our movements, such as drawing the curtains when we awake, chopping the banana for breakfast, feeling the water on our skin in the shower, can connect us to our senses and bring a slower pace into our day as we savour these sensations. It is this slower pace and allowing ourselves to be enriched by our senses that can bring us much pleasure and connection to our environment. Mindfulness covers various exercises, including focusing on one sense at a time – for example, noting one sound and listening to that. This really anchors the mind in the present and stops it from wandering all over the place. It can also connect us to the spirit within. (See *Exercise 8* for an exercise on listening to our bodies.)

It is through the senses that the 'inner eye', an ability to see things from a different perspective and have a newness of vision, is developed. I am able to notice things that connect to 'me' much more, which enhances who I truly am. Symbols and images help me make sense of who I am and how I belong in this world. The fallen tree, the solitary flower, and shapes and colour can all resound somewhere inside me. 'Your eyes are windows into your body. If you open your eyes wide in wonder and belief, your body fills up with light. If you live squinty-eyed in greed and distrust, your body is a dank cellar. If you pull the blinds on your windows, what a dark life you will have!' (Matthew 6:22-23, *The Message*). Using the visual sense, really looking at things around us, to reflect on the personal journey can bring a deeper richness to life.

Jesus said, according to Luke 8:18, 'Consider carefully how you listen' and this is a continuing challenge for me. Using the sense of hearing to unfurl the inner ear needs a reflective stillness to be aware of the depth of sounds around. It starts with an outside listening and notes what resonates with the personal journey. There is a story I once heard of a job interview where the people applying for the job were waiting together in one big room. There was a hubbub of chatter whilst they waited to be called. An announcement was made after a while that someone had been appointed for the job. There was puzzlement as no one had been called for interview. It was explained that, while they were waiting, a message had been tapped out in Morse code. One person had heard this and had reported the message, and so he got the job. As we listen there will be sounds that mean something to us, that give us a message to be heard. Listening to external sounds can also take us out of our internal dialogue, the self-talk that can sometimes encroach too much on our lives.

I find a lot of pleasure comes to me through my senses. Smells and touch are lovely ways of connecting me to the present: lemon peel rubbed on my hands, aromatherapy oils sprinkled in the bath, the wind on my skin, the texture of the rough bark and the solidity of a wall. They give me a sense of self, another way of connection to where I am in the present moment. They seal and enlarge the experience for me and I can understand why Keats wrote the line: 'Touch has a memory'.[33]

I enjoy stitch and textiles, and I once did an experiment where I let my senses lead me to develop a piece of textile art. I went into my store of materials and threads and just noted what I was drawn to. I picked out a piece of green material and some threads and found that I knew how to start. As I developed the first few stitches, it came to me what I wanted to do next. I did no planning, no thinking it all out, just let myself be drawn to what felt

---

33. John Keats, 'To _.' (What can I do to drive away) – see https://ebooks. adelaide.edu.au/k/keats/john/poems/to--.html for full text.

right. I continued adding different colours, stitches and buttons; I even found a title for the piece came to me as I stitched. At each stage I knew what I had to do; it was a very exciting process for me. It became a precious piece of work – not only did I realise that somehow I had this knowing within me, a way of going through a piece of work, but also the piece became a link to God, a meditation in itself. When the piece was completed I had something that told me a lot about myself as well as confirming that I could trust in following the next steps with God. Proverbs 3:19 talks about the understanding and knowledge of God by which the heavens and the earth were created, and it felt that this sewing experiment was somehow connecting me to this understanding: a way through life where there is a sense of knowing each step of the way.

The senses can develop this knowing, the voice of which could be called intuition: sensing the best direction to go and choosing the way that is right for the true self. God leads in different ways, allowing a stretching and sense of space. We need to be open to our senses, to listen to the body, to connect to these ways.

An evening I spent on a course on 'Personal and Spiritual growth' at Worth Abbey one year centred on listening to our bodies. We went into the Abbey to let our bodies lead us and to express what they wanted. I had been hurt by something someone had said to me that day and my mind was still chuntering about it. As I wandered through the big circular abbey interior I came to a small, dark area. I found myself lying in front of an altar in a foetal position and, as a small child again, the tears came. As my body acknowledged this hurt, I started noticing what was around me: the architecture of the ceiling and the lovely cloth draping over the altar with a wonderful texture. Then I found my body wanted to get up and walk around and I was led from this dark area into the light of the main church. There I was moved by the beautiful flowers, the light reflecting off the water in the baptismal bowl, and by the solid texture of the brick wall. I let my body move in a way that expressed what I sensed. This was a very moving process for me. I was amazed at how my body processed what had happened to me in the day, expressing the hurt and moving on to delight. I have allowed my body to lead me in many different ways since then. If I feel confused or emotional, I note how my body wants to express this. Does it want to sink to the floor, be prostrate before God, or walk slowly around the room?

We can use our body to change our mood and bodily functions by finding better positions and habits. I recently read that people who have had Botox injections around the eyes and lips are not as happy as they were previously, as they cannot smile so well. Not only do we smile when we are happy but it also works the other way round – if we smile the body becomes happier. The way we sit and carry ourselves also influences the body. The spine contains the spinal cord, a bundle of nerves that carries all the information from the nervous system to the brain. The cerebrospinal fluid contained in the spinal cord has its own energy and rhythm that can be very much affected by stress and fear as well as by poor posture. It might seem out of place to include notes on posture but it is all part of how we care for our bodies and carry ourselves and may make a big difference to our connection to the path of life. Having a more upright, open posture with no tension in the neck or back can help oxygen to reach the organs and the spinal fluid to circulate, with an accompanying positive influence on our mood and health.

I worked with someone who suffered from depression and anxiety. She loved to dance, and so one session I got her to show me how her body would express her anxious thoughts. She whirled her arms around and said it reminded her of a Catherine wheel with her thoughts scattering all over the place. I asked her what her body (rather than her mind) wanted to do and she started doing gentler, flowing movements. I then suggested she listen to what God was saying to her body. She dropped to the floor and lay there prone (for quite a while!). She felt God saying to her to let go and to have peace. Her body was showing her a way to override her scattered and anxious thoughts. She also explored the difference in how her body expressed sadness and happiness. The slumping position of the depressed body she could actively change to a straighter, more open position if she chose. This would help her be aware of her situation and bring about more positive emotions, maybe even releasing more difficult emotions.

Our bodies can give us clues to what is going on behind the scenes of our lives through our emotions as well as our energy levels. Noting what revitalises or saps our energy can help us understand the body. If I am doing a task where my energy flows well or one that energises me, then I know that I am connecting to my gifts and what suits me. When the body relaxes, feels excited, is emotionally moved, or laughs, then this can show us our passions and a better path. By noting when my energy is low and what thoughts, relationships and situations have led to this, I can review my life and whether there is anything I need to change. The body may also be highlighting a need to rest and be nurtured, especially if it has gone through a period of expending energy. There will be a balance of rest and activity that is right for each individual. Energy is a powerful key to noting what is happening to us in life (see *Exercises 9a* and *9b*).

I have been seeing someone regularly for the last few years who helps me with my energy levels, working on the acupressure points on my body to help the flow of my energy. She describes the energy in our body as having channels like rivers that flow through our body, and the work she does as keeping the river banks clear of silt so the energy can flow well. It is something that

I can practise on myself and I find it very healing. It is helpful in waking up my body in the morning, in clearing headaches, sorting my digestion and generally managing my energy levels in a better way. There are many practices around that help with energy levels, such as tai chi and Jin Shin Jyutsu (the type of acupressure used on me). The organisation Capacitar International connects energy and emotional work and has a comprehensive list of helpful acupressure holds, breathing exercises and other tools for wellbeing.[34] Their website explains that medical professionals studying the impact of trauma on the body now recognise that the human brain is composed of a 'cognitive' brain responsible for language and abstract thinking, and a 'limbic or emotional' brain responsible for emotions and the instinctual control of behaviour. The emotional brain controls much of the body's physiology, autonomic responses and psychological wellbeing and contains natural mechanisms for self-healing. Many emotional disorders seem to be the result of dysfunctions in the emotional brain and this can be reprogrammed using methods that act on the body.

Our energy levels are key indicators of what is going on in our thoughts, emotions, spirit and physical health. The system in our body that keeps us healthy and prevents infections is the immune system. This is made up of a network of cells, tissues and organs that work

---

34. See http://www.capacitar.org.

together to protect the body, defending us from germs and microorganisms. For this huge process to work as efficiently as possible we need to work with our bodies to help sustain its functions. There are many things that can suppress this system and affect our energy, from stress to excess sugar. We can care for our immune system through this room, listening to our body and finding its right pace. There are many nutrients that support the system, such as those found in garlic, ginger, fruit and vegetables, and when the system is struggling we have the option to take supportive products, such as a good multivitamin, extra vitamin C or a zinc supplement. Colostrum tablets are also a good natural product to aid the immune system.[35]

We are made very aware that our body is struggling when we suffer from illness. This can take so many forms of pain and fatigue. The skin and the digestive system are big indicators of unrest and imbalance in the body. The skin is the largest organ of our body and aids in the elimination of the waste products of many bodily processes carried in sweat through the pores. It receives a third of all blood that is circulated in the body, so it will be a good indication of what is going on in our bodies. When our skin shows signs of imbalance or distress, it will be telling us of toxins, allergies or a struggling immune system. Saunas, steam rooms and dry brushing

---

35. See http://www.patrickholford.com and http://www.gutdoctor.com.

the skin are all ways of helping the skin rid itself of toxins (provided the skin is not broken). Dry skin brushing can aid the breakdown of unwanted toxins, encourage cell renewal and stimulate the nerve endings.[36]

The digestive system fluctuates with the demands on our life. There are 100 trillion organisms living in our gut and these can easily get out of balance. We can note if our waste is easily passed or whether we need to adjust our diet to achieve better elimination. Fibre from a healthy diet is needed for our gut; linseeds (or flaxseeds as they are also known) are especially beneficial for the smooth elimination of waste. Bacteria that help keep the gut healthy can be found in certain yoghurts and kefir.

The body needs our tender care, time to rest and relax, for tensions to resolve. It needs us to think of appropriate rewards and time that will give it its due care. Being aware of the impacts in our daily lives can help us to bring about this care and a greater respect for the body, which has difficulty healing when tense and stressed. Having some relaxing walks, pampering, a bath or massage, for example, can help maintain focus on caring for the body. There are many relaxation exercises that can assist the body to relax, especially before sleep. We might like to thank our body for all it does and give it an occasional pat on the back.

---

36. See http://www.mindbodygreen.com/0-7955/why-you-should-start-dry-body-brushing-today.html.

The libido is a good thermometer of the body's energy levels. This could be defined as the physiological and emotional energy associated with the sex drive but Freud, who originated the term, also saw the libido as linked with all constructive human activity. Carl Jung broadened the term to encompass all life processes in all species. Our sexual nature is a powerful energy within us that can easily get squashed by life's demands, and the state of our libido is a good indicator of our connection to the path of life. When we are connected to this power, we are also connected to our deepest desires. The Roman Catholic priest Ronald Rolheiser states:

> Sexuality is a beautiful, good, extremely powerful, sacred energy, given us by God, and experienced in every cell of our being as an irrepressible urge to overcome our incompleteness, to move towards unity and consummation with that which is beyond us. It is also the pulse to celebrate, to give and to receive delight, to find our way back to the Garden of Eden where we can be naked, shameless, and without worry and work as we make love in the moonlight.[37]

The libido is not just about an urge for sexual gratification, or a connection between two people, but a force that helps us to overcome our fears of absorption, opening up our feelings and allowing more intimacy with our

---

37. http://ronrolheiser.com/a-mature-sexuality/#Vf-5599Viko

own bodies, as well as coming into a more intimate relationship with God. The sacred energy will bring an increased love for humankind and other aspects of God's creation. The theologian and scholar Philip Sheldrake mentions that when we allow ourselves to become aware of our sexual desire we gain important indicators of the deeper and more complex levels of our existence. This awareness offers the possibility of growing into maturity not only psychologically but also spiritually.[38]

Two main symbols of our sexuality – the womb and the phallus – can help us understand the application of the libido. The womb is a vessel for protection and receiving; somewhere for being open to the incoming seed – to new ideas, which may lead to new life. The symbol of the seed bearer is the phallus which is worshipped as a source of life in many cultures. It is seen as the channel for the life force and, through its hardening or softening in the presence or absence of energy, as a balancing agent responsible for maintaining equilibrium. I see this symbol as representing an energy and excitement linking the outer world to the individual's inner world. The womb needs that channel, a sense of something from the outer world, a connection to community and love, for example, for there to be an interaction of the seed and the egg to bring forth new life.

---

38. See Philip Sheldrake, *Befriending our Desires* (Darton, Longman & Todd, 2002).

I know that personally I need to be aware of my libido in order not to fear the channels of life that God is showing me. The outer world can be threatening at times, particularly at times of change. Fear tends to close me up and make me introspective, but if I am aware of my libido, of what excites me, of where my desires are pulling me, then it helps me to overcome my fears. For me to connect to this sacred energy, I find I need a certain amount of openness, a relaxing, a connection with that 'turned on' feeling, so that I can flow with life and be open to intimacy and what that brings to me. Sexuality is about exploring beyond the boundaries of the self; it is about spontaneity and an abandonment that means letting go of control. Connecting with the power, the libido, can enable this new life.

The body is the vessel containing the sacred, communicating to us through emotions and the senses, through non-verbal, creative ways. It is very much the vessel for coping with life on earth. Looking after this vessel takes care, and exercise can help with this. Findings from the Health Survey for England (2007) suggest people believe they are more active than they actually are. Only 6 per cent of men and 4 per cent of women met the government's current recommendations for physical activity by achieving at least 30 minutes of moderate or vigorous activity on at least 5 days in the week, accumulated in bouts of at least 10 minutes. It can be a struggle fitting exercise into the day, and yet the body really needs stretching and moving for its maintenance. Physical activity allows for the release of emotions and any stored adrenaline. Exercise can free any blocked energy that might be causing problems in the body or mind, as it releases chemicals in the brain that help manage pain in the body and mind and can lead to a 'feel-good factor', which is why exercise is suggested to help with mild depression. Finding an exercise pattern that suits is key to being able to keep it up. Laughing while you dance, jogging with a friend, stretching to music, rambling in nature, finding a rhythm while swimming – whatever motivates you is important.

Jesus' body was one that was destroyed and then raised up after three days; it was a place of resurrection. As the body ages, St Paul encourages us not to lose heart: 'though outwardly we are wasting away, yet inwardly we are being renewed day by day' (2 Corinthians 4:16). There is a sense that whatever state our body is in, there is a way of inwardly getting stronger through the connection with the divine – a taste of resurrection here on earth. It's easy to get discouraged by the problems from our body through ill-health and disability, but it may be by listening to the body through these problems that we can get a better connection to the inner spirit and to different gifts in ourselves.

Paul describes our body as a tent on earth that, once destroyed, will be replaced by a heavenly dwelling, and there can be hope in this thought of a new palatial home.

We can't know exactly what will become of us, but we can read of Jesus' new resurrected body in the Gospels and Paul's thoughts in the letters to the Corinthians.[39] Tom Wright comments that Paul describes heaven not as the place we go to when we die, but rather as the place where God has our future bodies already in store for us.[40] However frustrated we get with our bodies, there is the thought that there is a place where we will experience no pain, worries or tensions, and will maybe get a new body that functions in a very different way.

For Consideration

- How intimately do I know my body?
- Have I explored my body and considered its processes?
- What are my feelings about my body?

Vanessa's Story

Vanessa had not really connected her body with any spiritual dimension before. Doing so made her feel a bit more proactive in trying to care better for her body. She was unhappy about having put on weight over the last couple of years, but knew it was because she had

---

39. 1 Corinthians 15, and 2 Corinthians 4 and 5.
40. See Tom Wright, *Paul for Everyone. 2 Corinthians* (SPCK, 2014).

become more frustrated with life. She liked being in the retreat where they gave you three meals a day and there was no way of snacking in between. Vanessa had been encouraged to spend a morning in the spacious room on her own. As she put the 'Do not disturb' sign on the door, she felt a flutter of nerves about what she was doing. At home there was no big empty space; in fact, she had no space she could call her own, sharing a bedroom with her husband and other rooms with all the family. So here she was, faced by a large private space. She didn't know what to do; she had been given no detailed instruction apart from to focus on her body and let her body lead. Her body felt a bit heavy and lumpish but she started to slowly walk around the room, touching the walls, feeling their roughness and solidity. She took off her shoes, letting her socked feet slip and slide on the cold linoleum. Her body had not had her focus for a long time, but now she was really trying to connect and to listen to what it might want to express and what it might need. Her body bent down low and then started to stretch with arms up high. With joints creaking, Vanessa began to enjoy the opportunity that this room was giving her – freedom to move, to do a funny walk and to express herself. She started to laugh, a whoop that escaped and led to a shout. Up and down, round and round she twirled, with loose arms and a wide grin. This was what her body needed – space for expression – and she spent a long time relishing this, finishing in a heap on the floor, still and relaxed, bathing in her experience. She felt as though she had been freed from restraining chains; she felt alive.

Mike's Story

Mike was reluctant to do anything about his body, as to him it was full of frustrations. It had not been right for a couple of years now and had led to him leaving work. He peered round the door of the spacious room one day to find it free, so he decided he would just spend a very short time there and see what happened. He sat himself in front of the mirror and took a good look at himself. He noted the drawn face and the greying hair and found himself asking this person why it was looking so old and tense. 'I am trying to protect you,' came the answer; 'you are full of fear and uncertainty so I am geared up to hold you together.' Mike was surprised that an answer he imagined from this reflected body had come so easily. He was also shocked by its content. He knew he had never really got to the bottom of his bad nights and the tightness he felt in his body, but he was angry with his body for causing him so much aggro. He found himself telling this body in the mirror all about his annoyance. The body replied: 'You are angry and I feel that anger, it is bouncing around inside me. You need to express this out of me. You have got to this state because you have ignored me.' He asked the body what he should be doing. 'Listen to me and work with me. I can tell you things from another perspective.' 'OK, then tell me why I am so tired?' Mike asked. The body replied: 'I am weary because you are a lost traveller and I don't know what I'm doing. You need to set up a good structure for me and take me into account when you do the things you do. You tend to plough on regardless of me telling you I'm tired. I do that for a reason so that you stop and consider me.' It had just never occurred to Mike to try and work out what his body was telling him, and the conversation continued for a little while. He then found himself sagging back on the floor with a big sigh. The sigh felt good and he took a bigger breath and sighed it out. When he did this a third time, he found a noise emerging with the sigh. It felt as though it was coming from a deep place. He continued making some noises from deep within; it felt like a release of all his tension and anger. He started laughing at the sheer absurdity of what he was doing, but at the same time he knew it felt good and he sprawled out, feeling peaceful and relaxed.

The Creative Room

Using creativity to explore the life-giving path

'It is the creative potential itself in human beings that is the image of God.'

Mary Daly [41]

This is a large, airy, light room with plenty of surface space on which to create. The cupboards are filled with creative materials including paints, brushes, crayons, clay, plasticine, glue, papers, magazines, needles, threads and sparkles: a whole array of colourful and inspiring materials. There are cleaning facilities by the sink. This is a room where there is freedom to play, to explore one's path through creative media.

Mrs Mole was a wonderful character developed by Ronald Searle and I enjoyed a lovely exhibition of Mrs Mole's happenings some 40 years after they had been completed. The cartoon drawings depicted Mrs Mole pottering about doing domestic chores and busying herself in and around

---

41. Mary Daly, http://www.brainyquote.com/quotes/authors/m/mary_daly.html.

her house in Provence. The caricatures had been created during a really desolate time for Ronald when his wife had been diagnosed with cancer and given a pessimistic prognosis. This was in 1969 when chemotherapy was in its infancy. Each time his wife went for this treatment Ronald would produce another drawing of the calm and contented Mrs Mole doing the things that his wife enjoyed. His wife survived her ordeal, probably very much encouraged by Ronald's love and creativity. When I saw this exhibition I was struck by the way Ronald had used his natural gifts to console. He remarked that he only had his talent for drawing and so he drew. The drawings comforted and encouraged his wife over the six years she underwent treatment. She said she would lie in bed, living the life he created in the pictures. Both artist and recipient found a way through this painful time through creativity. The drawings that had been so private and personal were now being revealed and would go on to delight and inspire others such as myself.

Creativity has a way of drawing us to the path of life, whether it is through our own creative output, or by pondering on the creativity of others. Dr Sarah Law has stated: 'It is my experience that many people have a longing to express themselves creatively, and to explore others' creativity, and that this longing is part of a larger need to know one's authentic place or path in the world.'[42]

---

42. Dr Sarah Law, in a lecture entitled 'A Room of Her Own: Julian, Prayer and Creativity'.

Connecting to our own creativity helps us to find a way of expressing our inner needs and emotions and to find a perspective and enlightening on our path of life. The creativity of others also produces responses within us that help us unravel our complex paths. Poets, artists and musicians can be a great help to fuel our imagination and awaken inspiration.

This is a special room in the retreat designed to activate our natural creative selves and inspire an interest in play and creativity to help connect to the path of life. Connecting creatively uncovers symbols, images and thoughts that can really help us understand our personal journey. The word 'create' comes from the Latin 'creare', meaning 'to bring forth', implying that creativity is about self-expression, nurturing something into life, not about achievement or doing something to a certain standard. Connecting to my own creativity has been an exciting way for me to find out more about myself and my faith, spilling over into fun and entertainment in life. No more am I bored when standing in a queue or stuck in a traffic jam, as there seem to be so many shapes and colours that catch my eye!

Our creativity begins functioning in the last trimester of pregnancy and is operational at birth. The right hemisphere of our brain sees things whole and in patterns, so babies can start to recognise faces and comprehend non-verbal communication, engaging creative skills before language develops. In a few left-handed people the functions are in the opposite hemispheres, but generally this right hemisphere functioning sees through imagination and pictures and is linked to our emotional being. Through this right side we can understand how things exist in space and how the parts go together to make up the whole; we can comprehend metaphors and dreams and create new combinations of ideas. The left hemisphere does not start operating fully until the second year of life when language begins to develop. This left hemisphere houses the functions of speech and language; it comprehends words and sentences and stores verbal memories. It works through logic, reason and detail. When we are being creative, we are not only firing up the right hemisphere of the brain but, according to recent research, activating the whole brain – left, right, top and bottom – as the activated cells have longer neural branches and more neural connections than the left hemisphere.

Opening up the whole brain allows us to access areas of our unconscious that the left brain function cannot retrieve. Our memories, emotions and repressed parts of our life can only be accessed through creative channels. Creativity introduces a vast inner landscape that is open to us to explore and to find the gifts that it offers. A good example of this is the use of images, metaphors and symbols which are pivotal in connecting the two halves of the brain. They can sum up very complex thoughts and needs, so allowing a deeper understanding of our life (see *Exercise 10a*). During a walk I took while on retreat one year I was struck by an image that connected to my situation. It was a fallen tree – probably felled in the hurricane of 1989, with half its roots still in the ground. It had been able to continue growing, although with a horizontal trunk it had a lot of boughs shooting vertically. The main trunk, from ground level, had managed to merge into the roots of another felled tree, so supporting another life. It told me much about my situation – one where I had been knocked over years before, yet that felling had given me the ability to grow in a different way, to fruit different boughs and support other felled trees. I sat on that tree for quite some time, while it revealed a summary of my life.

There are different speeds of brain wave for the various brain functions. Part of the reason why our creativity is often inhibited is the way our minds have been trained. Constantly activating the left hemisphere – through stimuli such as phones, computers, television, studying and verbal conversations – tends to generate the faster beta brain waves. Our minds are often conditioned to be in this state of high arousal with lots of activity. It is like having our minds driving on fast straight roads. Bringing in creativity uses roads that are longer and more winding, slowing down the brain waves to bring the alpha wave pattern into play. This is a state of non-arousal – the state our brain is in when we unwind, break off from work and go for a walk, for instance. This is a good state for our brain, opening out areas so there is connection with emotions and an ability to visualise. There will be mental clarity so that we are more receptive to learn. We will have less anxiety and an ability to tap into pleasure and humour as well. Most importantly, this slower and more winding road state is a good condition for the body, mind and spirit to heal. It is very difficult for healing to take place if our brain is speeding down those motorways.

So for creative thoughts to happen there needs to be less visual stimulus and a decrease of the high beta rhythm in the brainwaves to a slower alpha rhythm through mental relaxation. Having times in the day when our minds can drift or we can daydream, for example, will allow for openings of creativity. My view of housework has improved since I realised that this can be a good time for creative thoughts to arise! Creativity can also be enabled if we break up regular routines and habits – by, for example, turning off the computer or television or walking a different way to work.

Music can also stimulate the whole brain. Alan Yentob in a television programme about how music affects us was given a brain scan while listening to Jessye Norman singing his favourite aria. This was one that stirred his emotions and, as he listened, his whole brain lit up on the scan; every bit of it was engaged, which was really amazing to see. Chanting such as Gregorian chant is growing in popularity, and scientists have shown that its particular rhythm integrates the processing information of the right and left hemispheres of the brain. Music can not only be a pleasure, but can also have a dramatic effect on our thinking and emotions.

Getting more connected to creativity needs to start with do-able small steps such as noticing what attracts us. Seeing what catches the eye, what stirs us, and what sounds and textures attract will inspire us and tell us more about our journey. When choosing clothes to wear it may be that we notice the colours and the textures; when reading we may notice a particular word or phrase that stirs; when shopping it may be that a particular item makes us look twice; we may notice particular lines and shapes in the ordinary that draw us and seem aesthetically pleasing to the eye.

Colours can have a real impact on our lives if we open ourselves to their richness. Being aware of what colours we are attracted to, what colours we wear, the use of colour in the everyday, will speak to our individuality. Flicking through a magazine and connecting with colours (rather than words or pictures) can be an interesting exercise to notice what those colours are saying about our present situation. I have explored colour with emotions, noting with each emotion what colour and shapes connect to it (see *Exercise 10b*). Colours connect to and reveal our mood; they can also change our mood and be a positive influence. Imagining or looking at colours which appeal, like the brighter colours, can create a better mood. I once saw an experiment in which people were asked to go into a red or blue tent, and inside each tent to estimate the length of one minute. In the red tent people timed one minute fairly accurately, but in the blue tent they added an average of 11 seconds to the time. They were more relaxed in the blue tent, losing the sense of time. Perhaps we all need that blue tent in our homes!

Journaling is a good way to express something of these creative noticings. The journal can become a space, not to note just the surface events of daily life, but what has resonated, touched us, produced the laughter, hurts, frustrations and tears through our daily happenings. Writing on a blank page (as lines can be restrictive), maybe with different colours, can help with these insights. We can write our questions, express feelings, listen to our thoughts and use poems and Bible passages as a base for rewording our experience – all onto the page. Using the non-dominant hand can also be revealing. Each half of the brain controls the opposite side of the body. So the left hemisphere controls the right half of the body and vice versa. Using the non-dominant hand facilitates the creative brain and can enable further insights.

If we have an intense response to something, it is good to seize the moment and get something down straight away. For example, if our anger is stirred then letting it out on paper can be helpful not only in calming things down, but also in attaining some insight into the anger. The journal provides a place of freedom to explore, a place where the personal journey can be noted and re-read. Threads will start appearing that can be linked to form a bigger picture of ourselves and our faith. *Exercises 11a–f* are short exercises for the journal.

Once stuff from within comes out onto the page it can be seen and worked with. It is much easier to realise what is happening and find out why if it can be highlighted and explored. It is also there to note and re-inform in the coming months. Opening up our innate creativity leads to an exciting journey; symbols and thoughts tend to link to each other to form a more integrated whole. Reflecting on something that draws us may then link to a memory, which might go on to link to something we read in a book, for example. The other day a phrase I heard on television reminded me of a symbol that had occurred for me during a reflection-time a few months before. It was a symbol that I wasn't clear about at the time and I was able to go back in my journal to understand its meaning more completely. There was a sense of the pieces of my jigsaw slotting together.

In my book *Finding Your Inner Treasure* there is a much fuller explanation of creativity.[43] I have included many tools for sparking creativity, from journaling to creative writing and art, as well as using these to explore all different aspects of life, so this might be a useful addition if this is a room that interests you.

---

43. Helen Warwick, *Finding your Inner Treasure: A spiritual journey of creative exploration* (Kevin Mayhew, 2010).

Crowhurst Christian Healing Centre is a lovely retreat centre in East Sussex. They have prioritised a building in the garden for a creative space where people on retreat can explore their journey. When I have run retreats there, I have been very careful to try and dispel fears and myths around the word 'art', so that people can be freed to explore. Many people have blocks that stop their creativity. School art has a lot to answer for, as people have been put off ways of creating due to their created work not fitting the expectations of teacher and syllabus. Having to create something that looks like an object or to pass a test is very different from expressing something from within. Some people have an ideal of what they consider creative, and it usually involves thinking about great works of art, fashion or poetry. Once I have managed to assure people that everyone has an innate creativity, evident in the everyday life of working out what to wear and what to eat, enjoying a joke, or doodling whilst on the phone, then I am able to assist people to explore their journey. It is in that creative space in the art room that the most exciting processes go on that really enhance and enlighten each person's retreat. If an individual is able to stay in the moment, with their 'flow', and let the creation emerge then they are often excited at how the creative materials reveal what they are going through in a visual and tactile way. I also need to encourage people not to criticise what they do and to trust that what is happening is right for them. Their creations may seem infantile, and yet they usually have an amazing message to give to the person.

Tiredness can sometimes be a benefit when trying out creative exercises, as it helps to knock the logical left brain on the head. It is this logical side, wanting clear explanations, that has a loud voice in condemning and criticising the roundabout and mystical way of the creative brain. It can be very difficult to subdue, and will bring the hardest challenges to this room, finding all sorts of ways why we shouldn't take time out to imagine, or use our hands to write or colour. This is why I always reinforce to those I am working with to try and approach creativity in a relaxed way, getting stuck in without thinking too hard. Pausing to focus on the body by, for instance, connecting to the breath, taking a short walk, or just doodling, can also assist in connecting to the right hemisphere brain.

Even though I have been practising creative ways for many years, I am always amazed at what comes out of the paint, clay, magazines and words in that art room. One person came who had been many times before, but this time she felt like doing something different with her hands. I suggested clay – just to sit and squidge it around in her hands and to see what happened. What did happen stunned her – out of this lump of clay developed a very symbolic image that spoke to her of something very personal. Another person wanted to explore her anxiety. I suggested she take a large sheet of paper and on one side stick pictures and words cut from magazines that connected her to this anxiety. She could use the other side to place things from magazines that expressed the opposite – life without anxiety. When completed, this personal collage gave her a lot for reflection.

Doing an activity where we are using our hands to create is part of an important process of connecting our body and brain. Making is something our body has an innate capacity for, from right back to prehistoric times. Our hands and muscles are part of our consciousness and need to have periods of being used for creating. If we let our hands lead instead of our head in this creative room, then we are often drawn to great insights into our journey.

God has made us creative beings; we are made in his image. There is a real delight that comes through the way God creates. In Proverbs 8 we read of Wisdom who exists at the beginning of God's work. She is credited with nurturing and creative attributes. In verses 30 and 31 we read: 'Then I was the craftsman at his side. I was filled with delight day after day, rejoicing always in his presence, rejoicing in his whole world and delighting in mankind.' We can get a sense of this connection with the Creator through our expression of the creative – in colour, word, through our senses, in dance, in worship or just as a whoop of pleasure. As we awaken our creative being, we begin to grow into the 'artist' to be part of the continuing creation around us. We can then share in the ongoing act of creation, being co-workers with God, co-creating within this constant renewal of the world.

Bezalel is the first person highlighted in the Bible to receive the creative Spirit of God. He is chosen as a highly skilled craftsman to be involved in the decoration of the tabernacle, which is being made as a reflection of God's greatness and a recognition of the divine place amongst the Israelites in the time of Moses. 'Then the Lord said to Moses "See, I have chosen Bezalel . . . and I have filled him with the Spirit of God, with wisdom, with understanding, with knowledge and with all kinds of skills . . . "' (Exodus 31:1-3). This not only attributes a very high value to craftsmanship, perhaps very different from the present day, but it also reinforces the Spirit's influence to inspire and empower. It is often this inspiration that can lead to a better connection to the path of life and one's purpose.

Whilst David was a shepherd he learnt to play the harp. It was this music-making later on in his life that calmed the tormented King Saul and got David a job at the palace, leading to his eventual kingship. Creativity often reveals gifts, ones that we may be unaware of or have forgotten, that can be developed not only for enjoyment, but to connect to our purpose in life. With myself it was my journal writing and linking into creativity that led me to the way I work now as a writer and spiritual director.

This sense of delight and spontaneity found in God's creating can be seen so naturally in babies and children where there is an engagement and flow between the imagination, emotions and timelessness. Play is such a crucial element in development. Donald Winnicott, the psychoanalyst, believed that the practice of childhood play was essential to the maintenance of a true self. His observations found that play could access the whole of a person's personality and, through the creativity induced by play, more of the self could be discovered.[44] It seems that even in adulthood much can be discovered by play. Having times in our lives where we forget the usual structure of the day and see what flows, letting some spontaneity in, can be a revealing and relaxing time (we may need a child to lead us!). Play or recreation is about re-creating, it restores perspective and brings about a balance and integration into our lives. It is about giving ourselves space and allowing ourselves to let our hair down and have fun.

There are moments when the creative brain is engaged when time seems to fall away and we can become utterly absorbed in the present activity; such moments have been observed by the psychologist Mihály Csíkszentmihályi.[45] He names this state 'flow' and proposes that we are happiest when concentrating as much as possible on something that's both quite hard and for which we have an aptitude. It is these times of flow that open up the right

---

44. D.W. Winnicott, *Playing and Reality* (Tavistock Publications, 1971).
45. See http://psychology.about.com/od/PositivePsychology/a/flow.htm.

side of the brain to allow the whole brain to connect. It is a state of living in the moment, a joy-filled moment, and it occurs in different ways for different people, depending on our skills. Some might experience flow whilst engaged in a sport or walking in the hills, or in other activities such as painting, drawing, writing or singing. Prayer and meditation can also open us to flow-times. Whether it is in colouring or making a daisy chain, this sense of flow can come about even at times of illness, when there may be little energy. I found it enhancing during my chronic illness to find activities, however small, that absorbed my mind and had my energy flowing well. I could do these activities for far longer than others that seemed to sap my energy.

These flow-times are not often drawn into our lives unless we are incredibly fortunate to have a job where the work absorbs the mind and body at the peak of concentration and skill. When we do find these activities that connect us to the present moment, it is worth reviewing what keeps us in this flow and when this starts to change. For example, targets that are introduced to bring about some sort of achievement may affect the flow – as with a person who paints for pleasure but then tries to make it into a commercial enterprise.

The therapeutic use of creativity was brought to my attention when I did a person-centred art therapy course. It introduced many creative ways of exploring – bringing up symbols and images linking what was previously in an unconscious place to see its connection and relevance in the present moment. Week by week we would explore and gain insights into what had come up through the creative exercises, helping our self-awareness and developing our knowledge and practice. One of the exercises used the imagination. We were asked to imagine going into the sea and then diving under the water. Even though I knew this to be my imagination, I found that I was really resistant to this. Firstly, the sea I was standing in was really murky – the water looked decidedly unpleasant. Secondly, I was unsure how I was going to breathe and didn't fancy holding my breath. So I took myself off to a warm tropical sea where there was crystal clear water with beautiful fish swimming around and I was in fairly shallow water. Then it was easy to pop my head under the water where I found a shell that was particularly symbolic for my journey at the time. Once I was encouraged by what had come up from my findings, I was brave enough at a later time to tackle the murky waters. These too revealed a very personal offering and helped quell the fear of diving into my unconscious world. I enjoyed continuing a creative way of exploring, finding it gave me exciting feedback.

Encouraging the imagination is such a good step for opening out the creative brain. Whether it is daydreaming, visualising the day you have had, bringing up memories or having an imaginary conversation with inspiring people, it all encourages the creative mind. Imagination can also help us to focus on what we want from life. It is a strong tool for helping us move from desire to reality. It has been said that if you can picture it you can accomplish it. Scientists have shown that it doesn't matter whether we are seeing something for real, or whether we are imagining something – the same part of the brain is stimulated to produce the images in our mind. Using the imagination can give us positive images and produce the same reactions in our body as if what we are imagining was really happening. This is why having a collection of inspirational pictures to bring up at pertinent points in life, when needing encouragement for instance, can be helpful.

Using the imagination with our faith – for example, imagining the divine coming into some of our memories, pictures or dreams – can develop very interesting scenarios. Whatever we perceive as God's perspective can really change some of the difficult images we have in our minds. Using the imagination with the Bible can also be illuminating. Picturing the scenes or envisaging conversations between the people encountered as you read really makes the Bible a personal and revealing book.

Dreams can reveal the creative in its full glory. Almost all humans dream, although whether dreams are remembered depends at what stage of sleep the person awakes. People sometimes find that it is when they go away from their home – for example, on holiday or on retreat – that they experience a dream that sticks in their minds. The Bible portrays many dreams that reveal messages for the dreamer as well as messages to convey to others, endorsing that God communicates through the unconscious mind. Some dreams conveyed in the Bible have a clear message whereas others are symbolic, more obscure and need an explanation – for example, Pharaoh's dream in Genesis 41 that Joseph interpreted.

Getting a sense of the symbolic language of dreams can be difficult. Initially just noting the dream, maybe talking or writing it out in the present tense, can help to capture its flavour. Noting the emotions that are around and whether we have felt the same emotions recently can be helpful. Jung believed that each part of the dream (including people, objects and scenery) represents different elements of the dreamer – so that person I have just struck with my sword may be a part of me that is being injured. The sword itself could be a part of me that is doing the damage. It can all get rather confusing, but it is worth taking the initial step of noting anything that seems particularly significant – perhaps a dream that crops up repeatedly. The dream can also be used to enhance the imagination, perhaps by picturing what we might prefer to happen or what happens next. Imagining Jesus or a spiritual presence coming into the visual picture of the dream can sometimes bring another perspective on the dream, clarifying the message or assisting in how the dream might develop.[46]

---

46. For further assistance with dreams see Russ Parker, *Healing Dreams: Their Power and Purpose in your Spiritual Life* (SPCK, 2013) or Helen Warwick, *Finding your Inner Treasure*.

I had a couple of dreams that motivated me into action and to better health. The first dream was about being woken by a baby crying. I got up and followed the crying and found a baby trapped by the neck, between the cot and the wall. I was able to rescue the baby. When I thought about the dream it seemed important that, firstly, I woke up and, secondly, I rescued the baby. It encouraged me to wake up to my present situation and listen to what might need to change. I then had another dream that led me to think about the times in my past when I had had a lot of responsibility and stress. These past memories seemed to be part of a chronic tension, burdening my neck. I explored what I felt was happening, through writing, drawing a picture and talking with my spiritual director. The area around my neck had become somewhere to dump my worries, and realising that I was tensing the muscles around my neck and shoulders when stressed helped me to change the way I was reacting. I got some practical help with an osteopath and started some Pilates exercises and consciously tried to relax my neck and shoulders throughout the day. Interestingly, this has led to my being more relaxed as my body has no longer got its storehouse for the stress.

As part of the retreat, this room can help explore the other rooms. It is worth spending some time exploring and you don't need expensive materials, just a sense of discovery and an openness to notice. Tackle an exercise that appeals and you may be surprised!

For Consideration

- What do I do in my day that links into creativity?

- Are there ways I would like to be more creative?

- What might be stopping me having moments of play, spontaneity or using my imagination?

- Could I consider a container for my thoughts, writings and creativity, such as a sketchbook or journal, so I have them all in one place for reflection?

Mike's Story

Mike was quite excited about going into the creative space as he was realising that surprises were coming up for him in different ways. He was eager to try something with his hands. He was still feeling very unsure about his life and the direction it should go, but liked the thought of seeing what would happen if he just messed about in the creative room. He had a wander around, looking at the materials – of which there were many. He was drawn to the clay; he fancied seeing what would happen if he took a big lump of it. He sat himself by the large window, looking out onto the lovely garden and just started playing around with the clay. He appreciated the solidity of the clay and the way it felt in his hands. He rolled it out, watched the marks made in it from his thumb prints and found himself separating it into three blocks. Each of these he rolled around in his hands to make rough circular balls. The biggest of these he kept smooth but the other two he found himself pounding into with the end of a pencil. It seemed to be getting out some of his frustration, just sinking this pencil hard into the clay. He moved on to the smoother, largest ball and, as he moulded, a shape formed that reminded him of a bird. He had been enjoying watching the birds in the garden at the retreat. This bird reminded him of their freedom, but also of their purposefulness in life. It seemed important that this clay bird had a nest of some sort, so one of the pummelled balls he rolled out, enjoying seeing how the round circles of the pencil stabbings stretched and made beautiful patterns. This 'nest' he cupped round the bird. The last piece of clay seemed poised to be made into an egg. He rolled it again in his hands and decided to make it into two eggs for the bird. When he reflected on what had gone on for him, he was impressed by what had developed. Out of his messing about and getting rid of his frustration, a scenario had built up that he really related to. His new redundancy did give him a certain freedom, but with his poor health he felt his wings had been clipped. The importance of the nest for the bird made him reflect about stability and how he could set up his home and his life to enable this. The eggs reminded him of new life and made him think of what his responsibility was at the moment – maybe to create a life that connected somehow to God and his community. He took the clay pieces back to his room for further thoughts.

Vanessa's Story

Vanessa was nervous as she approached the creative room. Having got so much out of letting her body lead in the spacious room, she wanted to see what would happen if she allowed the same in this room. However, her nerves got the better of her and, on being faced with all the different materials, a sense of panic rose within her. One of the staff members, Miles, took her aside and, after Vanessa had mentioned her panic (which was a familiar, but very unpleasant sense to her), Miles suggested she connect with this feeling by taking some crayons and seeing what came out on a sheet of paper. Thus after a few minutes Vanessa had in front of her a mess of bright colours that seemed to sum up her panic within. It was difficult seeing it out there facing her. It made her more aware of that churning feeling inside. She didn't know what to do about it, so she turned to Miles for some help. Miles suggested she describe what had happened in making the picture. Vanessa had noted how she had been led to certain colours and how some shapes seemed flowing and some jagged. The red especially she had wanted to really press down hard onto the paper and had ended up shading in a large area. Miles helped her talk through some of these feelings that were coming out on the paper – the yellow seemed to have an active vibrancy about it, while the red reminded her of her procrastination, and the black connected to her fear. She realised that her panicky feeling was made up of different things, maybe to do with her difficulty with making decisions and with her fear of failure. She wasn't sure how some of these thoughts had come to her but it felt good trying to sort out what was happening in the panic. Miles asked her where she would be in the picture and she knew straight away that she was right in the centre, surrounded by this swirl of colour. She was then asked to imagine what might happen to the picture if some divine presence came into it. Vanessa thought of all the colours swirling around her and imagined a calm light resting onto the swirl. It made the colours seem to sag and start to flow downwards, like warmed wax melting. She took another piece of paper and drew out the displaced colours, lying in a gentle swirl in a pool. This time she introduced some other colours – purple seemed important to place around this pool. She loved the way the picture was developing and just wanted to take it back to her room and reflect on it on her own. It felt special in some way, especially alongside the first picture.

The Dining Room and Lounge

Connecting with our identity and exploring the life-giving path through relationships

'I must look for my identity, somehow, not only in God but in other men.'

Thomas Merton [47]

There are two main rooms in the retreat where people can interact. The dining room has circular tables that can seat six people, allowing each to be heard during the mealtimes. The lounge is a large, but cosy room containing comfy settees and individual upright chairs. These are rooms where people can relax, hear each other's stories and share their experiences.

Jean Vanier is well known for setting up the L'Arche communities after being made aware of the plight of

---

47. Thomas Merton, *New Seeds of Contemplation* (New Directions, 2007), p.51.

people with learning disabilities through his friendship with Père Thomas in France. The latter was a priest who taught much to Jean Vanier and in 1964 Jean opened his house to two men from the local institution, one of many that kept those with learning disabilities locked up in conditions that exacerbated their problems. Those first beginnings have led to the development of many L'Arche communities all over the world. The concept of each community is that the abled and disabled live together in homes. Their roles merge as they become fellow humans together who share care and need. Jean found that he started becoming fully human, more of a whole person, when living with these vulnerable people, as they were showing him sides of himself that he couldn't reach without them. The learning disabled were gifted in relationship, and were people of the heart and of trust. They had the capacity to reveal areas which the abled found really difficult, such as weakness, vulnerability and dependence, and it was through these areas that people were being transformed.[48]

Here in the dining room and lounge of the retreat we meet others that may encourage or provoke our journey. This part of the retreat considers the relationships in our lives which can be a help or a hindrance, but which often show us about ourselves and enhance our path of life. As Thomas Merton mentions in the opening quote we

---

48. See Kathryn Spink, *The Miracle, the Message, the Story: Jean Vanier and L'Arche* (Paulist Press, 2004).

need others to be able to understand our own identity: they provide a mirror for us to see ourselves. On our own we may choose an identity that covers up areas that we don't want to face, maybe wearing a mask that only shows the areas we want others to see. In these rooms we can consider our identity and how God and others can input and strengthen that identity. Love, with its ability to transform, is highlighted as an important aspect of these rooms.

We discover our own connection with our self, our awareness of our own identity, through relationship with others. When we are babies, the mother-figure is the key relationship and, as we grow, other relationships become important such as those with family, peers, friends, partners, significant teachers and inspirational guides. The psychologist Erik Erikson has delineated the eight stages of human development to cast light on how we mature and form our identity. He sees growth as a lifelong process with ever new opportunities to discover gifts for loving. His eight stages include development not just in childhood but throughout our entire lives, with strengths and weaknesses at each stage showing us some of the processes that are needed to obtain wholeness. Erikson believed that development missed earlier can be made up later, and that anything can be healed. So if we had problems with the key mother-figure as a baby there may be issues of trust with others and this can be worked on. The 'terrible twos' involves movement from the 'we' of baby and mother, to an 'I'. The child is learning something of its will. As the child goes into play age, it is starting to take responsibility for itself. If there is a sense of failure and guilt around this, the child will be less likely to take initiatives. Adolescence is another crucial phase, a time of learning about personal strengths and weaknesses. There can be a reluctance to accept the new self. Problems at this stage can lead to great confusion with identity. The challenges in adulthood can be met through doing something new, or doing old things with new insight, and having models of other people who have dealt successfully with this stage. Even into maturity Erikson outlined the need for acceptance of oneself and one's life, and the integration of these elements into a stable pattern of living. If this is difficult, then this stage can be associated with self-contempt and fear of death.[49]

Reflecting back on the different stages of our lives can help us to review the relationships we had, where community was for us, and the strengths and weaknesses at each stage. I moved house at the age of six, from the south to the north of England and started a new school in the summer term. My sister and I were the only children in the school to be wearing summer uniform that first day of term! A few months on and my elder brother was moved to a boarding school, as my parents were not

49. For Eric Erikson's Stages of Psychosocial Development see Matthew Linn, Sheila Fabricant and Dennis Linn, *Healing the Eight Stages of Life* (Paulist Press, 1988) and also http://psychology.about.com/od/psychosocialtheories/a/psychosocial.htm.

satisfied with his new school. This was something that had much more of an impact as my relationship with my brother was drastically altered. I ended up working through this impact much later on in my life. In Erikson's model the school age is where a child should become less self-centred and learn to give and take. Problems at this stage may mean the child develops a sense of inferiority, of not being good enough. With me, I think it linked in to needing to achieve and work hard, especially with changing from the middle child to an eldest sibling during term-times. This has had both strengths and weaknesses as I have matured. It can be a help to our own journey and our relationships with others if we have spent some time (maybe with the addition of the listening room) on thoughts of our own relationships from the past and their effect on us (see *Exercise 12*).

Our most key relationship is with ourselves. This retreat where we are stepping back and observing ourselves, who we are and what our hopes and desires are, should be making a strong relationship with ourselves – finding a faithful friend within. Our paths can lead us through lonely times and finding this friend, our true self, can be a comfort and nurture. This is a friend who will speak with compassion and who is intimately connected to God and the love offered. Connecting to others through your true self, from this stable place, a place of humility and strength, will enhance your relationships and enable others to find their true place.

As we observe ourselves it is interesting to note the different aspects of ourselves. These aspects can be noted as adjectives, such as weak, strong, controlling or likeable, and include moods such as happy, sad, excited, flustered. They can also be noted as characters, such as the child, policeman, leader, victim, parent, lover, wise person or soldier. These words can all help to describe the different parts of us, each a part of a detailed mosaic that together make up a whole. The more we find out about the different parts of ourselves the more we will be able to form a relationship with ourselves and feel a sense of this whole. I have a box of collected objects – plastic animals, shells, toys and other intriguing pieces – which I use to help others to explore aspects of themselves. When I picked out things for myself, I chose a shiny ring which represented my core, connected to my treasure and to the divine. I also had a chatty tortoise that ploughed on at a regular pace through life, a piece of tinsel that represented my creativity, a paperclip connecting to the part of me that holds things together, a silent lion and a cockerel that was the observer, looking over the rest of the pieces. Seeing all these pieces together highlighted their effect in bringing out a more unified voice; the voice of the chatty tortoise wouldn't on its own bring out the wisdom of the silent lion and aspects of the other pieces. I could connect to a more rounded and balanced voice when I was more aware of my different aspects. These might change and be added to when I became aware of other aspects of myself, but it was good to see what I was aware of at present. (See *Exercise 13.*)

Finding the different aspects of ourselves can also highlight the strengths and weaknesses of each part. When one directee explored the different aspects of herself she chose a few pieces from my box of objects. Some plastic flowers represented her caring side which she placed alongside her happy part and sparkling side. She knew that her caring side had strengths but felt it also had a major weakness, in that she often felt responsible for people and guilty that she hadn't done enough. She could see that when she became burdened it affected her happy and sparkling sides – they were lost. The little mouse represented her vulnerable side which she could see actually helped her caring. She also picked out a guardian angel figure and a cross. We talked about keeping a stability and balance with these aspects so that none of them became too dominant, affecting the other aspects.

It is interesting to note our own self-esteem and how much we value ourselves, as this is such an important aspect of finding our path of life. If we do not hold ourselves as precious and valuable, it is much harder to find a positive way forward; we may be unconsciously wanting a path that drags us down, as we feel that is what we deserve. We may have all sorts of issues in our past that have affected our ability to have a sense of self and be able to connect and value that self. There is *always* a chance to repair this. To explore and encourage our identity there are three aspects in our lives that we can consider. I see them as three legs of a stool, with each leg needed to give balance and support. The first leg includes our interaction with others: our families, friends, community and church. The second leg is the outside draw from the 'more-than-ourselves'; it is a leg that encompasses our purpose in life with meaning and hope. The third leg is the social one of giving ourselves to work we do for a living or for a vocational activity. These three legs, which will all be explored further, can be the supports that help us through life, incorporating friendship and community, giving and receiving, with the draw from our hopes, desires and purpose coming from a link to the divine.[50] (See *Exercise 14*.)

Our relationships and the communities in which we live are key components of our identity. This is the first leg of our stool where being connected to a group of people – in our families, with friends, in our neighbourhoods, in our work and in faith communities (and the wider community on the net) – offers us ways of becoming more fulfilled and whole. What we know at present of our inner mosaic of different aspects of ourselves has been revealed through the relationships we have had in the past and through our own reflections. This mosaic will continue to be revealed through our current relationships and situations. We will react in various ways

---

50. Based on the three pillars by the psychiatrist Dr Pablo Martinez. A series of lectures.

with different people – being shy, bossy, more animated, childlike, embarrassed, or friendly, for example. Many of these interactions we will be unaware of, but we can start noting what reactions we have to others so that we can become better equipped to know ourselves and to change the way we react to others, if needed.

Past relationships that have nurtured and infused comfort and love will have strengthened our identity, but relationships that have rankled, frustrated or abused will be just as much part of our mosaic, revealing aspects of ourselves. Jean Vanier said of the L'Arche community: 'It is in living together, in relationship to people, that all kinds of feelings well up inside me – frustration, anger, fear. So community is really the place of the revelation of my darkness. None of us likes to discover our jealousies, our fears, our depression, our need to be loved, our desire to be better than others. Community is particularly painful because it is the place that reveals my wounds, my own inadequacies.'[51] Any close community will know that the person who stirs up the most emotion within is the most effective at showing us our missing pieces. This stirred emotion gives clues to find hidden areas within ourselves that can be addressed, and the creative room will have further ideas for this revealing.

---

51. Quoted in Michael Mitton, *Wild Beasts and Angels* (Darton, Longman & Todd, 2000), p.113.

We need relationships to keep us on the path of life; it is a hard path to walk on our own. So it is worth considering the others we need and how we can go about finding them or developing the relationships we already have. Finding someone we know as a good listener to encourage a mutual sharing will be an invaluable asset, both for ourselves and the friend. We may want to deepen a current friendship or to find someone new. It takes risk to enter into a relationship where there can be more honest dialogue to allow a discovering and support of each other, but this can lead to vital strength in our journeying and will encourage our self-worth. It can start with a phone call or meeting and testing-out time, maybe leading to regular times together. Alongside a more supportive relationship, we may need others to support the roles we are in or to help encourage different aspects of ourselves. When the Virgin Mary was told that she was newly pregnant, she was encouraged to spend time with her cousin Elizabeth, which she did for three months. This was someone who would understand her condition and what she was going through and this must have been a pivotal three months for Mary, giving her the strength to go back to Joseph and manage the rest of the pregnancy and expectations of others. We might need to consider particular support at new junctures in our lives, which might not need to be for long or take too much of our time; sometimes a pertinent phone call or meeting can be of help.

I find the concept of a pie chart helpful in considering my relationships and the support I feel I might need in the different areas of my life (see *Exercise 14a*). It is too much to expect any one person to be able to help with all our needs and to support us in each of our roles. Identifying others who can support the different areas of our lives will help us reflect more of our inner mosaic. One directee who found this helpful noticed that one of her needs – that of having someone to understand her difficulties and give her a hug at times – was met when she viewed the circle as a whole. She realised that when she noted all the relationships she had in her chart, it felt as if she had had a collective hug.

It is interesting to see how our mosaics fit with those of other people. In our more intimate relationships there is the potential to create a new identity – one that joins various aspects of ourselves with aspects of our partner to reflect a special entity, bringing increased potential and creative possibilities. My sister, who works as a Relate counsellor, shared the interesting fact that people often partner the person who will make them more whole. We are drawn to the person who can provide the missing links to our lives (and this includes deep friendships that we form). For this to happen, there needs to be an openness and honesty and good communication between the two. However, what initially attracts us to that person is often what irritates us later on, as it is these things that are highlighting issues that need addressing within ourselves.

Nobody can really understand what it is like to be in our skin. It is hard enough for us to understand ourselves, let alone anyone else! It is easy to yearn for things out of our reach or to want others to change, instead of making the effort to change ourselves. A most helpful tool was shown to us early on in our marriage which was to speak from our feelings. How do I feel about this or that? I feel like this when you do that, or when this happens to me. Telling another how I react can help explain how I view the incident, which might be very different from the way they are viewing the same event.

Whether we are becoming more intimate with a partner or learning to be more intimate in our friendships, learning to love others and to cope with the risk, openness and vulnerability that can result is a difficult route, but one that will connect us to our path of life. Love is an amazing force that can enable us to see both the gifts and the potential in another. I like the phrase about learning to love the not-yet-beautiful. We need to value each other and learn to love the not-yet-beautiful in ourselves and the other person, and give each other the time and space for change.[52]

Another aspect of this first leg is the Christian community we may belong to, or would like to join. When two or three get together within God's love, there is a reflecting of our aspects with more creativity and power. There is a great sense in the Bible of all believers

---

52. See Clarissa Pinkola Estés, *Women who Run with the Wolves*, p.144.

being joined as a whole, described as the body of Christ. In community our identity should ideally be respected and encouraged. St Paul makes an analogy between the Church and the human body, describing how the identity of each individual has an effect on the health of the whole body, the body of Christ. 'God has put the body together, giving greater honour to the parts that lacked it, so that there should be no division in the body, but that its parts should have equal concern for each other. If one part suffers, every part suffers with it; if one part is honoured, every part rejoices with it' (1 Corinthians 12:24-26).

Alongside the human relationships that influence our lives is exploring the draw towards a relationship with the divine, representing the second leg of our stool. The psychiatrist Gerald May notes that somewhere within, at a primeval level, we desire to re-unite with the ultimate Source of being; this, May opines, is one of the four primary forces in human spirituality – that of our longing for the love of God. God's longing for us is the second force: God desires to express unconditional love and it is this that prompts our longing for God. Often it can only be seen in retrospect that we have been led to something that enlightened us.[53] I helped one year at the L'Arche community in Bognor Regis. This was as a spiritual director where all members of the community were

---

53. Gerald G. May, *Care of Mind, Care of Spirit* (HarperOne, 1997), pp.24-5.

being offered some time with a spiritual director during their week of 'retreat in daily life'. Those with learning disabilities in L'Arche are called the Core Members. I worked with one Core Member who, when I lit a candle to start our session. spent a good five minutes gazing in silence at the candle; the way she connected with the significance of that candle for her spoke to me. I was invited for tea each evening at one of the houses and was very moved by another of the Core Members who seemed to be always smiling. She couldn't speak or communicate her needs very well, and yet she enjoyed just watching the goings-on in the house, bursting into laughter when there was some action such as someone banging the table. Another Core Member would occasionally turn to her, pat her hand and say, 'You are happy, are you happy?' It was very touching to witness. The week at this community spoke so much to me of the love God has for all, and how this was reflected through the love shown by the carers and by all who were receiving this love.

God's love for us is a force that draws us away from self-centredness and gives us an increasing awareness of a 'more-than-ourselves', and this love and our own love for God are two positive forces that link us to the path of life. The third and fourth forces in human spirituality drag us away from this path of life. The third force comprises our own internal fears and resistance to this love and to our spiritual growth and will be explored in greater detail in the store cupboard chapter. It includes the many times we turn away from the love that is offered by God for whatever reason. This third force is also apparent if we look for relationships to boost the ego and make us feel good about ourselves or to satisfy a need, rather than coming from the stability that our true self brings. The fourth force I will be noting further in this chapter.

We need to hear what God is saying into our being, as well as hearing input from others. Clarifying our own identity is difficult if we use only our own reflections and psychology; we need inspiration and input from the 'more-than-ourselves' which is a calling to an intimate relationship that supports and reveals our identity. There is much in the Bible about God's attitude towards each individual – that we are each precious, honoured and loved. Are we able to hear God's acceptance of us? Can we hear 'I love you, you are my precious child' from the Spirit within? Hearing ourselves being affirmed by God is often hugely difficult for people (see *Exercise 15*).

This second leg – the relationship with the divine – is complex and is explored in different rooms in this retreat. The following illustration is something that came to me about letting go and being drawn into God's love. Let me take you abseiling. Imagine the person on his first lesson on top of a rock – one that is high enough for a bit of vertigo. The instructor has given his talk and strapped him into a complex harness. Now comes the time to launch himself off the rock. He is sweating, his body is screaming not to go; it was not made to launch into thin air at a ridiculous angle. It takes him an age to lean back on the rope, to feel its pull, and take courage from the instructor. He steps one foot off the edge and then the other, so that he is leaning right back, straining at the rope. His only focus is on the rope, his feet and his fear. He keeps stepping down and back, feeding the rope through his hands and hearing the instructor reassure him, until he comes to a shaky fall at ground level. What a relief.

I have only been abseiling once but I can relate to many terrifying experiences in my life where I have had to launch myself off rock faces and trust the instructor and rope that I grab. We can only take so much instruction from others, the Bible or other sources; it is up to us to take the step of faith into the unknown. The life-line with which God assures is that great love for us, and as I have ventured out onto the path of life I have come to feel its firm hold – like an umbilical cord, tying me to the Spirit. I try and look for this love, the times when I have felt held, loved and drawn closer to God, and note it in all its many ways. Love is the holding in faith, it is that connection, that life-line that attaches firmly to our identity.

As the abseiler continues to learn how best to launch himself off the rock face, he learns more about himself, the correct technique and what holds him. Each time he abseils it is a little easier, and by the time he has had his tenth lesson he has come to realise the experience enlarges every time. Now as he descends he feels the solidity of the rock under his feet, he notices the little plants that grow in the nooks and crannies of the rock and admires their beauty. He looks behind him at the stunning view and enjoys the exhilaration when he bounces on and off the rock, being in control with his hands and feet. He appreciates the relationship he is forming with the instructor and the knowledge he is learning about all the equipment, so that he can use this in his further exploits in rock climbing and abseiling. As the abseiler is learning about the whole experience and being enriched with each event, so in our life with God: as we keep launching ourselves off our own ways of control, we test out this life-line and see what we experience. Each time we rely on God, we learn more about the aspects of God that are offered. We hear the voice of the instructor, we test the strength of the rope, we start to realise that there are other aspects we can experience – the views, the exhilaration, the flora and fauna.

This scenario of the abseiler came to me in the middle of a night. After thinking it through, I fell asleep and had one of my rare flying dreams. These dreams, when I launch myself into the air and start flying unaided, are exhilarating and I always wake up with a sense of great excitement. This dream seemed to consolidate this illustration. As we venture to expand our relationship with God, we experience new areas. We test out and find new aspects of ourselves that also help us see new aspects of God. Experiencing flight with no ropes or instructions seems like a further step of faith for me.

As we have the capacity to form a new identity with soul partners, so in a relationship with God we find a new identity – that of the true self. I like the way nature can teach us so much about relationship and I note the symbiotic nature found so adeptly illustrated by lichen which reflects one of nature's fascinating relationships between algae and fungi. Separately they have their uses, but together they form a completely different being with many other functions. The relationship is very clever, the fungi providing protection for the algae and, depending on the degree of fungi or algae, numerous different lichens can be created that can survive in any climate in the world, from desert to ice. It has been thought that the manna in the desert may have been lichen blown by the wind, keeping the Israelites fed for 40 years. As God and each loved child form an intimate relationship, revealing that new identity of the true self, a powerful, creative being is formed that can do so much more together and has the ability to find the path of life in all diverse environments. This new identity we have in God is held as a stable relationship with the divine, and we can therefore approach others from this more centred position rather than from one skewed by our ego.

Love is something that we have to learn to receive, in order to be enabled by its strength and potential. When others are helpless, we are helped to grow through learning to love, but when it is we ourselves who are helpless, we need to learn to take on board the love that is offered to us. Receiving others' and God's abundant love needs openness and acceptance. When others pray for us, it is a joining of their love to God's love that is part of the strengthening and comfort of the prayer. Love has no need of an actual physical presence; we can receive love using our imagination and memory. We can picture loved ones, hear their encouragement and imagine being loved by God.

When a loved one dies, it leaves a deep hole within us that is filled with more pain than the benefits of love. Over time it is possible to be strengthened by the love of that person, by finding a way of accommodating our loved one in a new way in our life, whether by hearing their voice, or through good memories. It is finding a new place for them within us. Philip Larkin ended one of his poems with the words: 'What will survive of us is love', and I like the thought that, as our bodies deteriorate and leave this world, there is something of love that is left behind. Lois Tonkin, a grief counsellor, gives a good picture of the way that love can expand us as people, even through death. She describes a mother whose child had died as initially being completely consumed by her grief. The bereaved mother had drawn a circle to represent her life, marking her grief with shading which completely filled the circle. She assumed that over time the grief would shrink and become a smaller shaded circle within her. What happened was very different; she found that the shaded circle stayed the same size, and her life grew round her grief, making her life a larger circle.[54] There were times – anniversaries or moments which reminded her of her child – when she operated entirely from the grief circle, but increasingly she was able to experience life in the larger circle. Love and the grief that can result from the death of a loved one open us out to bigger experiences that cannot be learnt through study or books. It is the experience of love that connects to our knowing – our understanding and knowledge of ourselves and of God. It is something that cannot be obtained except through experience. As our knowing expands, with the sense of ourselves and the 'more- than- ourselves', so does our love.

The third leg of our stool is one through which we can strengthen our identity by giving ourselves to the work we do for a living or as a vocational activity. For the work to be a strength to our identity, it needs to be something that is done for fulfilment and which uses our gifts and talents. This trialling of our identity as we test out the different aspect of ourselves makes us more of who we are, and as we give out from our natural abilities we get feedback from others. Each of our inner aspects will need to be realised outwardly in some way for us to come to fulfilment. This will take us a life-time, as the different

54. From *Bereavement Care* Volume 15, Issue 1 (1996) – http://www.tandfon-line.com/doi/abs/10.10/02682629608657376?journalCode=rber20#preview.

aspects within are revealed, found and developed in the various seasons of our lives.

As unique individuals we will have aspects that contribute to our community and the good of the planet. Jesus modelled a whole life through giving out to others, especially the poor and the weak, from his life of togetherness with God and his disciples. Viktor Frankl in his reflections from Auschwitz could see that being human always points to something, or someone, other than oneself – be it a meaning to fulfil or another human being to encounter. He discovered through experience that the more one forgets oneself – by giving oneself to a cause or to another person – the more human one is and the more whole one becomes.[55]

The expectations of those around us, what our immediate environment is like and the people we live around can all contribute to our path, but they can also be an influence to pull us away from our path of life. Gerald May talks about a fourth force in human spirituality which comes from outside sources and may include worldly values and expectations that encourage ways of living that draw us away from God. This is a force we need to consider as we battle to find the path of life. These cultural and societal attitudes encourage us to think more of ourselves and desire things we don't need. We are constantly surrounded

---

55. Viktor E. Frankl, *Man's Search for Meaning*.

by news, adverts, opinions and temptations that tell us what we should think, buy and be like.

Added to these distractions may be the accommodation we need to make with our immediate environment. If we live in a turbulent area it may be harder to note the path of life if we get caught up in fear of what might happen to us. Whatever our circumstances, there will be elements we can use in that environment to make our home. I think of the lovely image of the caddis fly larva that creates a protective home for itself with whatever he finds around. This is a small worm-like creature found in rivers and ponds that is able to glue together tiny bits of sticks, stones and other debris found in its vicinity to create a strong structure around itself. The environment in which we find ourselves will offer ways for us to complete our own inner structures and be able to contribute our gifts, whatever our thinking and distractions are in that place.

There needs to be recognition of the pull away from our paths of life that relationships and community can cause, along with the realism that our bodies are designed to be part of a larger body of people. History has seen huge peaks in the need for community – during the two world wars, for instance. Nowadays community is just as much needed, especially for our mental and emotional survival. It was encouraging to read in a summary of news of 2013 that community spirit is making a comeback in our society. A large majority – 78 per cent of us – feel a strong sense of belonging to a neighbourhood; 72 per cent have volunteered formally or informally in the past year; and 50 per cent say they exchange favours with their neighbours.[56]

Each individual and their gifts contribute to completing the bigger community structure. If we take this into our faith communities, then each set of unique gifts is needed to build that Holy Temple, whether those gifts are seen in active or passive people, abled or disabled, helpless or helpful people. Our faith-filled communities need to be reflective of the inner structures of each person and to create a greater mosaic themselves to be a reflection of the area around each community. The fourth force that functions in opposition to spiritual growth also includes spiritual forces that can seek to pull us away from the life-giving path. There may be many names for these latter forces – the enemy or devil, for instance – and there is much to be found in the Bible and other writings regarding them. Being in community with people who support and pray with us in our journey can help with the discernment of these forces.

The Bible is concerned with the wholeness of a community, the life to come being a large part of our community here on earth. We can be part of a Holy Temple that connects to all those gone before us.

---

56. See https://www.gov.uk/government/collections/community-life-survey.

The writer of the letter to the Hebrews describes those faith-filled people as 'a great cloud of witnesses' that can encourage us to persevere with the race marked out for us.[57] Prayer can link us to this vast, encouraging community. Like the love that can be experienced even if the person is not living, the encouragement and strength from this community can also be tapped into to help us feel more whole.

Jung did much study into our connections with each other, looking at the collective unconscious. He saw this as a deeper stratum of the unconscious than our personal unconscious, perceiving that our instincts and the way we react in certain situations must come from this collective part of our brain. He researched how the brain itself has been shaped and influenced by the experiences of humanity and reached the conclusion that we experience life in a way determined by our history.[58] Somewhere within us there is common ground with others, and I find there are circumstances where I am connecting with this ground. Having been through much suffering, I often have experiences of connecting to others' suffering – what I term as my suffering strand connecting to that strand in another. This can be through an empathetic moment or just a feeling, but there is a sense of connection to another. I have also experienced

---

57. Hebrews 12:1.
58. See Frieda Fordham, *An Introduction to Jung's Psychology*.

a moment that I compared to when Elizabeth met her cousin Mary for the first time since she became pregnant. Her own baby leapt for joy in her womb – the recognition of another and the deep communion of celebration. One of these moments for me was visiting someone after only an initial meeting and yet having this deep sense of mystery and joy within that get-together. Another way I am aware of this unity with others is through prayer and silence. I often go to our local Quaker meeting and there I have really experienced this sense of the solidity beneath my feet, connecting myself with the Quakers in the meeting and with all those outside of the meeting. It is a strong sense of stability – of God the rock under my feet, and of God being this bedrock that is the centre of the earth, being the solid ground of all humans. It is through this silence and prayer that I am aware of the bigger world around me and my connection as a small part of that world.

We all have our own individual story that can fit in with the bigger picture of community and God's Kingdom. Paul describes the Corinthian believers he was writing to as 'letters' from Christ, showing the result of his ministry and of their growth through God.[59] We are revealed as this letter – showing the relationships that have contributed to our inner structure and the influence of our community. As these letters, we can note what aids

---

59. 2 Corinthians 3:3.

our growth and how we contribute to the community. We can note what highlights our missing pieces and test the strength of our inner identity. Our letters and stories will contribute to the bigger picture of working together to affect other people's paths, as God qualifies us for changing people's lives.

For Consideration

- If I imagined the three legs of my stool would there be balance and strength or is there something I could work on to make it more stable?

- What were the important relationships for me in my past?

- Who were the people that reflected the love of God to me and who talked to me of God?

- What are the important relationships in my life now? Are there any areas in my life where I need more support?

- What do I see if I stand back and observe myself in my community? Where might the path of life be within that community?

Mike's Story

Mike had been enjoying his occasional stays at the retreat centre. On one occasion, Karen had asked him about significant people in his life who had taught him anything of love. Mike found himself telling her all about his sister to whom he had been very close at one time. He had tried not to think too much about her these last few years as she had died tragically of cancer when she was in her late twenties. He had deeply missed her and gone through a time of withdrawal from other people, just ticking along at work at a minimum level. Now he found he wanted to talk about her, and Karen listened as memories came flooding back. Karen asked about a positive memory he had of her and he recalled their times of sitting together, either in the garden or in one of their bedrooms, when they would set each other challenging questions, such as 'How would you cope on your own on a desert island?' or 'What would you do if you had loads of money?' He really enjoyed their chats and nothing had fully replaced the dynamic energy and bubbling personality of her in his life. There was still so much pain around for him when thinking of her. Karen suggested he imagine the scene of sitting with his sister and take time to remember, to perhaps try and talk to her and to listen to her words.

Later he was able to come back to Karen and tell her how helpful it had been to hear his sister's thoughts again. She had been such a strong love in his life and he was finding her voice again, asking him questions and 'listening' when he replied. He had imagined what she would say about his present life, and knew that she would be wanting him to not mope around at home, and would be encouraging him to make more of his life. He was able to bring these thoughts into his quiet times, just being with them in God's presence. It had given him the courage to find a course in woodwork, which he was really enjoying. He had also found out about the local monastery and had linked in to the meditation group they ran weekly. He was starting to get to know some of the people in that group, people who seemed to understand his way of wanting to connect to God.

Vanessa's Story

Vanessa was intrigued to see what would come of the exercise that her spiritual director had suggested where she explored her relationships in her life using a tin of buttons. She picked out buttons that she was drawn to when thinking of herself and the relationships in her life. Finding her own button was easy – there was a textured, cloth-covered button where the weaving had frayed, leaving wisps of cotton straggling over the edges. She placed this one in the middle of the table and then picked out ones to represent her husband and two girls. These she found were all overlapping her frayed button, giving her the sense of being slightly squashed and stifled. Other buttons appeared at various distances from her button – her two good friendships with other mothers she had kept in touch with from the local toddler group, and also the people in her church housegroup, some of whom she found a real support. She also placed buttons for other family members, a big one representing her aunt with whom she had a special affinity, and other buttons signifying some of the people at her workplace. Her spiritual director then suggested that she choose a button representing God. This she did, and this button was placed at the top of the table, overseeing all these relationships. She was fascinated when she saw all these buttons laid out on her table and took a photo of them with her phone.

After talking through the button image, her spiritual director suggested that she might review any changes in the formation. Vanessa knew immediately that she didn't want to be the button underneath her two girls and husband, but wasn't sure how this could change. Her spiritual director asked if there was any change that might happen if the God button was shifted. Vanessa moved the big God button to be underneath her. The husband and daughter buttons then had room to be around her on the God button, but not overlapping her. This seemed a more breathable position for her and she photographed that image too for further reflection. She also talked over her work relationships. Work was an area she was really reviewing at present as it wasn't stimulating her, but it was good to see how precious she found some of the relationships. They were making a big difference to her work environment. She took time at home to reflect on her relationships, her role as wife, mother and friend, and the support she was getting for herself.

The Library

Exploring the needs of the mind and finding a way of thinking that connects to the path of life

'If we do not develop our thinking the world becomes an unsafe and paranoid-making place. If we do develop our thinking, then the pain of all these different experiences becomes mitigated through our thoughts.'

Fiona Gardner [60]

This is a large, peaceful room, the walls lined with books. It has a circular table with seating, making a space for study and taking notes, and comfortable chairs around the room for relaxing reading time.

Apparently humans cannot do random. My son, a physicist, recounts that for research that needs random numbers scientists need the help of a machine to spit out these numbers. When I thought about this, I realised that if I tried giving random numbers I would give a limit to the numbers, finding all those below 100 for example, and go from high to low, and give different numbers,

---

60. Fiona Gardner, *Journeying Home*, p.100.

rather than the same. The machine, on the other hand, may spit out three consecutive numbers and be oblivious to the human mind's preference for set patterns and rules. The mind's affection for order can be troublesome when trying to work through the mystery of life – life where the clues are often in the random, in the chaos and mystery itself.

I have a special interest in how the mind works which stems from the various sorts of training I have had in the past, as well as from suffering various shades of health over the years. Keeping my mind in good health has become a high priority, knowing the devastation it can cause when thoughts are left to roam down paths that spiral down dark alleys. John Swinton, who has done much research into spirituality and mental health, says: 'If we are spiritually healthy we will feel generally alive, purposeful and fulfilled, but only to the extent that we are psychologically healthy as well. The relationship is bi-directional because of the intricate intertwining of these two parts of the person.'[61] In this quiet setting of the library there will be an exploration into the support needed for the mind and a reflection on the best state for our minds if we are to experience life to the full.

It is estimated that we use only a quarter of a per cent of our brain's capacity, its processing capacity being estimated at 2.5 million gigabytes. This amazing

---

61. John Swinton, *Spirituality and Mental Health Care*, pp.331-2.

three-pound structure processes information of immense complexity, brought to it by the senses, through its 100 billion nerve cells, each connected to between 25,000 to 100,000 others in a network. The result is an internal map of the external world shaped by each individual's perceptions. The conscious mind can only deal with between five and nine pieces of information at any given moment, so most of what is around is filtered out. The reality of what you see in the world can never be represented identically inside your brain, as there are many influences on what these pieces of information are, depending on how and what you filter. Values and beliefs, memories, decisions, experiences and your cultural and social background all have an influence on your filtering. I find it interesting to note in my own journey what my filters are, what information I notice and retain, and what completely passes me by.

Most people experience self-talk or automatic thoughts, although few are aware of this. What the thoughts say depends on our previous experiences and beliefs, but they are a way of interpreting the situations that face us. For many people the thoughts can be more negative than positive and can lead to a perpetual cycle of negative emotions that can be a block to making changes in our life. This voice can be a critical one that needles away, sapping confidence. Sometimes occasional thoughts may escalate and join with other thoughts. A starting thought might be: 'oh, I didn't do that very well' – but instead of stopping there, such a thought starts linking to others that feed this message and we end up concluding we are absolutely useless. At other times there may be repetitive tapes going on in the mind that have been set up in the past through experience but are actually not right. Examples may include: 'I must do everything perfectly or I will not feel good'; 'I am unattractive'; 'failure is a sign of weakness'; 'I should help everyone who needs it'; 'I am no good at this or that'. These beliefs we have set up for ourselves can become a filter through which we see the world. The mind can get stuck in various thought processes; it can replay images, traumatic events and past conversations incessantly. How many of us have been awake at night, replaying images from the past or worrying about something in the future? So it is worth noting our own self-talk and the reactions it may produce on our mood and body. (See *Exercise 16*.)

The Transactional Analysis (TA) model was developed by Eric Berne in the 1950s.

> Berne's hypothesis is that people form a 'Script' which is essentially an individual's belief about who they are, what the World is like, how they relate to the World, how the World relates to them, and how others treat them. Psychologists theorise that an individual forms their Script by the time they are four or five. A Script is based on what an individual is told, what they experience,

and how they interpret these external stimuli from their own internal frame of reference.[62]

This Script is often the basis of our self-talk. Berne suggested that each of us unconsciously contributes to or causes situations to occur to promote the beliefs in our Script. He reckoned that 99 per cent of people have a negative Script with limiting beliefs. By noting what our self-talk is and observing our mind we can go on to challenge ourselves as to whether our Script is leading us on a path of life, or whether it is dragging us down a difficult route.

I worked with someone at one time – let's call her Gillian – who was brought up by a very critical father. She learnt to expect criticism all the time. Even when she did something well, praise was short-lived and she often felt crushed. As an adult, even after her father had died, the same pattern of thoughts still went on. Any time something went wrong for Gillian or she felt misunderstood, she felt this crushing presence. The different challenges that happened in her life she always interpreted in the same way – that she was no good, useless, and not worthy of being loved. These thoughts made her want to hide away, to 'disappear'. This spilled over into her relationship with God and she felt she had a big black cloud blocking her path to receiving love.

---

62. See http://coachingsupervisionacademy.com/thought-leadership/the-karp-man-drama-triangle/.

Damage to our sense of value and self-esteem can have lasting effects on our thinking and behaviour.

The neurons that take messages all over our brains tend to go in set paths. Certain thoughts will trigger particular routes – they become automatic thoughts that run this route. Our thought patterns form our mindset, so we may have automatic thoughts that keep us in a negative mindset, which may be continually dragging us down a difficult path. It is difficult to change our neural pathways, and we can see this when there is change in our lives. When we face issues in our lives with new factors to take on board, new neural pathways will take time to be developed. Part of the stress and tiredness involved in a change in job or house, for instance, will arise from the fact that there are a lot of new stimuli confronting the brain. Things become easier when they are more familiar, so we can shut off to some of the stimuli. The presence of loved ones makes up part of our neural pathways, so part of our grieving process when something happens to them will be the brain adapting to these difficult new circumstances.

The good news regarding our thoughts is that the brain is malleable and constantly changing. It is possible to create new neural pathways in the brain, to develop new habits, thoughts and abilities even into old age. When I started to observe what was going on in my mind, it was a revelation to me that I could choose my thoughts, what I may keep in there and what I could chuck out.

We have choices

Chapter 1
I walk down the street,
There is a hole in the pavement, so deep.
I fall . . . call out, have no voice,
I didn't realize I had a choice,
It takes forever to find my way out.

Chapter 2
I walk down the same street,
There is a hole in the pavement, so deep.
I pretend I don't notice at all,
Again I fall,
As I do I begin to find my voice,
I begin to realise I have a choice,
It takes a long time to get out.

Chapter 3
I walk down the same street,
There is a hole in the pavement, so deep.
I clearly see it.
I fall in out of habit.
My eyes are open,
I have found my voice,
I have a choice,
I get out immediately.

Chapter 4

I walk down the same street.

There is a hole in the pavement so deep.

I walk around it.

Chapter 5

I walk down another street.[63]

It takes time to let go of our patterns of unhelpful thinking and to introduce new ways. We need to first be aware of the patterns and pathways our brains follow. Neuro-linguistic programming or NLP helps people to understand what makes them tick – how they think and feel and make sense of everyday life. It centres on a variety of techniques, stemming from renowned psychotherapists studied by Richard Bandler and John Grinder. Bandler and Grinder contend that beliefs are the generalisations we make about our life experience (they are not referring to religious beliefs). These generalisations go on to form the basis of our reality which then directs our behaviour. Bandler and Grinder suggest a limiting belief is present when words such as 'can't', 'should', 'shouldn't', 'could', 'couldn't', 'would' and 'ought' are used. When we are children, teachers and parents can impose their beliefs on us, but there needs to be the flexibility as an adult to be able to weigh up the pros and cons of the advice we were given and see whether it remains relevant for life at

---

63. Adapted version by Anon of 'Autobiography in Five Chapters' by
    Portia Nelson.

present. Beliefs can be self-fulfilling prophecies, so we need to choose which ones we want to hold onto. They develop into our ethical and moral standards. If these are too high, then we will fail all the time, so they need to be reviewed. We can challenge and change unhelpful ideas or beliefs. What this means is that we have control over the way we choose to experience our world. We can choose to change our mind to make a good time more pleasurable or to remove the negative emotions from an unpleasant one. It can be hard to change the state of the mind, but just knowing that there is a choice to reflect on life in a way that gives meaning and joy is a good motivator.

Changing the old thought patterns into more life-giving ones does not depend solely on positive thinking. Sally Brampton in her excellent book on depression writes that positive thinking tends to drive you straight at the wall – an impenetrable barrier in the thought processes. She found that the sort of thinking you need is working out how to be able to negotiate around the wall. It is a way of thinking that acknowledges and faces up to your obstacles and is open to a way around them. She looked at how she was brought up and realised her obstacles stemmed from not sharing feelings and learning to 'adapt', to be the good child. Part of her negotiating was to learn to express feelings and not to keep them bottled up.[64]

---

64. Sally Brampton, *Shoot the Damn Dog: A Memoir of Depression* (Bloomsbury, 2009).

The story that Jesus related regarding sheep and their shepherd sheds a light for me on reviewing thoughts. In the Gospel of John, Jesus tells how sheep are able to recognise the voice of the shepherd who leads them into the freedom of the pasture from their sheep pen. He starts by explaining how the shepherd is recognised: 'I tell you the truth, the man who does not enter the sheep pen by the gate, but climbs in by some other way, is a thief and a robber. The man who enters by the gate is the shepherd of his sheep. The watchman opens the gate for him, and the sheep listen to his voice' (John 10:1-3). I can relate to myself as a sheep and to the idea that I need to listen to the voice of the shepherd, a voice that belongs to one who can guide and nurture. This is a voice that is found within myself and can easily be drowned out by my own twittering voice. If my mind is busy with thoughts, then it is much harder to hear the voice of the shepherd. It is said that when we are stressed we lose 80 per cent of our hearing. To be able to listen to the voice of the shepherd, the voice that leads us on a path of life, we need to have a mind that is settled and open to be able to hear.

In the passage from John the watchman opens the gate for the shepherd he recognises. Eastern sheepfolds had only one door, which was guarded either by the shepherd himself when there was only one flock or by a watchman when several flocks were enclosed. In the latter case the watchman would know the shepherds. I like this idea of someone who is there observing and noticing who is the right person to direct the sheep. This is the observer, and it is this position that I find so helpful in noting what is in my mind and the reaction my body and mood have to my thoughts. I can be the watchman and observe which thoughts lead me to recognise that inner shepherd – thoughts that lead me to more energy, to a better life. There is a lovely verse in Proverbs that reads:

> Blessed is the man who listens to me,
> Watching daily at my gates,
> Waiting at the posts of my doors.
> For whoever finds me finds life,
> And obtains favour from the Lord.
>
> *Proverbs 8:34-35 (New King James Version)*

The writer of Proverbs encourages us to watch that gate – making sure that we keep focused on letting thoughts in that bring us closer to hearing the inner spirit.

The sheep are being protected and cared for in the sheep pen by the shepherd who leads them to life. Jesus goes on to say: 'I am the gate; whoever enters through me will be saved. They will come in and go out, and find pasture. The thief comes only to steal and kill and destroy; I have come that they may have life, and have it to the full' (John 10:9-10). The shepherd often slept in the sheep pen, by the opening, to protect the sheep from harm. To have this full life that is offered, the sheep need to 'come in and go out, and find pasture'. We have the picture here of Jesus being protector of the sheep but also someone who leads the sheep out of the protectiveness of the pen into the freedom of the pasture. That is the normal routine for the sheep – out in the pasture during the day, back safely in the sheep pen at night. This seems a continuing illustration connected to my thoughts. When I am aware of having thoughts going round and round in my head, or thoughts that lead me down a negative route, then I feel I am being restricted. It is as though I am stuck in the sheep pen and not able to get out into the pasture. When my thoughts are connected to the bigger picture – to the open pasture that God calls me to, to a better way of living – then it is easier to get through the day; I have that freedom to move and appreciate life. Thoughts that get our minds in a tangle restrict us from the life that God is offering us – life that is full. I know that when I am worrying, for instance, I am prevented from appreciating life – the worrying colours my view and bars me from noticing the good things.

The sheep pen is still important as a protective structure for the sheep. With regards to our way of thinking, we need to have a structure or container for our thoughts to be held and developed. As we grow older we need to grow out of the structured processes of the sheep pen and acquire a different way of thinking. This entails noticing our thoughts, especially the ones that seem restrictive or negative. The brain requires a way of holding thoughts that is flexible for transformation and change to occur. The dimension Jesus brings in as the gate to the sheep pen can be helpful for this transformation. This is a dimension that requires a trust outside of ourselves; it requires risk-taking to go through an open gate, but the pasture provides much space to explore our true self and to think outside the restrictions of the sheep pen. The pasture leads us to a new way of thinking.

Children who have had a difficult start in life, who have suffered childhood trauma and attachment issues will have had difficulty with forming an actual container for their thoughts. They will need help in forming a way of thinking that can hold thoughts and beliefs. The opening quote by Fiona Gardner is from a book she has written for those who have had childhood trauma and find it hard to connect to faith. She says that thinking involves a move from a formless, chaotic state, to a state where coherence is found and, with this, a new understanding. She sees that therapy can help with this coherence where there is opportunity to think through our actions, feelings and responses and this will be addressed in the next room. Once this ability has been established, it is much easier to open the mind to some sort of belief or trust – to reach out into the unknown.

The open pasture with its space to explore reflects a way of thinking that Jesus encouraged through story and image. When the disciples did not understand a parable, Jesus said: 'The knowledge of the secrets of the kingdom of God has been given to you, but to others I speak in parables, so that, "though seeing, they may not see; though hearing, they may not understand" ' (Luke 8:9-10). His statement suggests that it is only those people who have opened their internal eye and ear, thus opening up the mind to reflect on the bigger picture, who will be able to understand insights from the parable. There is a deeper knowledge available to each one who is able to see and hear in a different way.

We need the experience through the senses to connect to this deep knowing within, alongside symbols and images that are found in the Gospels, our dreams and in creation around us, to help explain this knowing. This experience needs to be brought alongside our logical, rational thoughts for us to be able to articulate and communicate our experience. It is both the experience and the rational, both sides of the brain, that need to be employed for a way of thinking that connects to the path of life.

Richard Rohr talks of these different ways of thinking as dualistic and non-dualistic.[65] Dualistic thinking is the linear thought, related to words, the logical and rational, coming from the left side of the brain. It is good for study and education and relates to the sheep pen in my illustration. Dualistic thinking can be black and white and very literal, whereas non-dualistic thinking flows from the creative brain, accessed through the senses, connecting left and right sides of the brain. It is a thinking that is complex and relates to the open pasture

---

65. Richard Rohr, *The Art of Looking Sideways* (CD from talks at Greenbelt 2010) – http://www.greenbelt.org.uk/media/talks/contributor:richard-rohr/.

way of thinking. *Exercise 17* gives some meditations for exploring this thinking. Real life, our everyday experience, is non-dualistic. We need both types of thinking to be able to connect to our experience and be able to make sense of it.

Integrating both the left and right sides of the brain with dualistic and non-dualistic thinking leads to a more coherent sense of self. Iain McGilchrist states that in the West the left brain has become a tyrant that insists we only truly understand things when we break them down into their constituent parts and process experience in a left brain sort of way. He challenges this notion, stating that the right brain's way of understanding is essential for a full comprehension of life, the universe and everything.[66] Richard Rohr adds to this by noticing that there are five big areas that cannot be understood by dualistic thinking alone. These are huge areas that our logical minds cannot grasp – those of love, death, suffering, God and the notion of infinity.[67] They all draw us to experiences outside of ourselves. Opening up the mind with the pasture thinking and using contemplation and creativity can help consolidate the experience of these areas. Both these activities help open the right hemisphere of the brain and slow the mind to the pace of the body.

---

66. Iain McGilchrist, *The Master and His Emissary: The Divided Brain and the Making of the Western World* (Yale University Press, 2009).

67. Richard Rohr, *The Art of Looking Sideways.*

St Augustine said that if you comprehend it, it is not of God.[68] What we have around in our minds is what we understand, whereas God works in the mystery, the secrets and hiddenness of life, experienced through non-dualistic thinking. I find this helpful when I often find myself questioning life – wanting to understand and have answers. Knowing that God is in the non-comprehension and that somehow what is happening is drawing me to the porthole of God helps me cope with the uncomfortable. It can be an opportunity to discover these secrets of the kingdom of God, finding more about myself and these five areas that could not be encountered through dualistic understanding. The new way of thinking accepts reality as it is; it is a mind that is able to view what is happening in a non-judgemental way, noting responses and being open to listen.

Another way that Jesus had of developing people's pasture thinking was to ask questions. Questions are much more important than answers as they send us searching. I was reminded the other day of a story of a man wanting to train as a minister. He took himself off on retreat, not to find out whether this was the right decision for him, but to find out whether he was asking the right questions. It is interesting to see what questions are around for ourselves at present. Deep questions

68. Sermons on the New Testament (Augustine), Sermon 2:16 – http://www. newadvent.org/fathers/160302.htm.

help us to develop a sense of meaning to life and give a motivation for this exploring.

There are many books on helpful ways of changing our thinking. Some of the tips that I find useful are the following :

- Being aware of the effect of my thinking – is it helping my life or hindering it? Am I getting what I need? Can I brainstorm and think around things, expand the way I think?

- To note that I am in control of my thoughts. There are many unwanted thoughts that will pop into my head but I do not need to heed them or act upon them. Thinking them does not mean that I will follow their lead. Thoughts are like seeds – if they get attention they will grow bigger and stronger.

- If there are thoughts that lead me down the difficult path, then I can see if there is evidence to support the thoughts and what alternative views there may be. For example, I might think about what I would say to a friend if she had these thoughts. I might also find a different perspective by thinking how Jesus or a wise person I know would tackle these thoughts.

- Unwanted thoughts can be stopped by using the stop technique. When I notice the thought, then saying 'Stop' and doing a physical sign with my hand – like holding it up – and then connecting myself with my senses can be helpful. Using the body reinforces stopping the thought and then connecting to the present moment – noticing the ground beneath my feet, what I am touching, seeing and hearing – brings the mind to a place where it can focus on what is happening. This is also the place where it can listen to the inner, wiser voice.

• Looking at the outcome of the thoughts – for example, considering what is the worst that could happen and how bad that would really be can help us to face the fear that some of our thoughts can bring.

One of my directees had as her top tip 'Don't even think about it' which had been the most benefit to her way of thinking. When I was suffering through chronic illness some helpful advice was to 'not think like an ill person'. My way of thinking had incorporated ways to negotiate life through the least energy available. I told my body when it should be resting and was fearful of repercussions if I changed the routine. If I was going out I would plan when I could sit down and the route that would take the least energy. These all came from practical strategies, except that all the planning was telling myself that I was ill, so it was setting my neural pathways down a route that kept me in ill health. I had to learn to think like a well person – to take each day and the needs of my body that day and to cope with the limitations in a way that didn't get my thoughts stuck down this particular route.

Gerald O'Mahony is a priest who suffers from bipolar disorder. In his small book *Finding the Still Point* he talks about how he notes his thoughts and moods so he can keep himself balanced. He compares his thoughts, energy and moods on a scale of one to ten. He notes that he is at his best between four and six, stating that our God-given calling keeps us at this midpoint, that he names the still point. This is when we feel at our healthiest and also closest to God. When his thoughts start to drag him down a difficult path where he feels low, he notices that they have dropped below four on the scale and he needs to find ways of righting that. When he finds his thoughts becoming too fast and he is doing more, he knows he is starting to increase above six on the scale and needs to find ways of slowing down.[69] We can find our own healthy point where we feel our minds function in the best way and where our energy flows well. We might need to find ways of noting when this healthy point is tipped to make our mood or energy low or too high and how we need to right ourselves, or bring ourselves back to this still point.

The library is somewhere that has many books that can help with guiding a new way of thinking. We need to find the books that connect with our own journey – which may be different from the books our friends are reading. Being open and listening whilst we read means that we can note what resonates. Whenever we

---

69. Gerald O'Mahony, *Finding the Still Point* (Eagle, 1996).

feel a reaction when we read, whether it is read in the newspaper, in a text book or a novel, then that is the place to stop and reflect. A verse from Isaiah highlights an aspect of listening: 'He wakens me morning by morning, wakens my ear to listen like one being instructed' (Isaiah 50:4). This gives the impression of a student being aware of what is going on around him, so he can pick up the information that God wants to reveal; a sense of listening avidly to what his master has in store for him each day. If we listen avidly, we may have more of a sense of the guide who is teaching this new pasture way of thinking.

We might also learn from new methods used in some primary schools for preparing the mind by connecting to the body. Before their study, children are taken through some physical exercises to connect both left and right sides of the brain. These use the body to track from the left to the right – for example, by tracing a large infinity symbol with the finger in front of the body. These exercises are meant to help the brain open up other areas so the children are aided in their studies. There are similar exercises in pilates and tai chi that help coordinate the body and link left and right sides of the brain.

Statistics show that one in four of us will suffer some sort of mental illness during our life-time, so it is worth observing the mind and taking care of it. The mind uses a lot of energy and needs pacing, just as the body needs to keep to a rhythm. Some of the mental states now being seen in the Western world are due to an overload of information to the mind. If there are times of concentration it is good to stop at regular intervals, to rest or to switch to physical activities, to keep the mind in a good state.

Considering what we put into our minds can be a huge influence in keeping ourselves on this path of life. As the conscious mind can only deal with between five and nine pieces of information at any given moment, it is worth reviewing what is put in front of our minds as there is so much influence around us. If we wake up to Radio 4 news every morning then how does that influence our mood and our day? If we continually watch or read about murders and violence, how do we process what we have seen or imagined? Having times of no television, radio, computer or phones can sometimes be revealing as to how much they influence our lives. I prefer to receive news through written sources as I find I have more control of what goes into my head, rather than watching the news on television which dictates what I see.

Changing the way we think takes time as the mind will want to revert to its well-worn tracks, but the more the new thoughts are practised, or old thoughts discarded, the more the brain will make those better tracks linking to a new-found life. Romans 12:2 says: 'Do not be conformed to this world, but be transformed by the renewing of your minds, so that you may discern what is the will of God – what is good and acceptable and perfect.'[70]

---

70. New Revised Standard Version.

For Consideration

- Do I notice what thoughts float around my head and what reactions they produce in my body?

- What voice dominates my self-talk? Is it a voice that is leading me to the path of life, or is it a voice that is critical, blaming and maybe dragging me down?

- What am I receiving or putting into my mind? Does this need reviewing?

Vanessa's Story

Vanessa went into the library to peruse the books. It was such a treat for her to have time to read. She noticed there was a section with books about Cognitive Behavioural Therapy. She had talked to a friend who had been on a Cognitive Behavioural Therapy course and had been especially helped with realising that her thoughts lay between what happens and her feelings. Vanessa knew there were ways that she could change her anxious thoughts and she picked up a book on Mindfulness Cognitive Behavioural Therapy to have a flick through. A diagram caught her eye that showed how a difficult situation might trigger all sorts of automatic thoughts leading to emotions from these thoughts. The alternative part of the diagram was to bring in awareness of these thoughts and then it listed a few options of what to do with these observations, such as letting the thoughts go or talking them over. She took a copy of the diagram to look at further.

Vanessa had also been trying out reflection using a Bible story. She was challenged by the story about a paralysed man from John 5. She could see the pertinent questions from Jesus that got people thinking. 'Do you want to be made well?' was the question Jesus asked the paralysed man who was waiting by the healing pool. She put herself into this story. There was a sense of sitting by the pool just waiting for life to get better. She realised that the paralysed man was waiting for others to help him into the pool. How much did she rely on others to change her life? Vanessa could see that the mat the man lay on was his little rectangle of safety. She imagined her own safety mat, linking it to her comfort zone. She knew there were areas of her life where she could change but she was fearful and preferred the status quo. Vanessa decided to spend more time imagining herself in this story and to talk it through with Jesus.

Mike's Story

Mike was finding that in his silent times interesting things were happening. He was able to note his thoughts when he was still. When they popped into his head he was more aware of them and he found it a powerful experience to not engage with these thoughts but just watch them. It made him feel in charge of himself somehow. He found that interesting memories were coming to him that were helping him remember special things about himself. He was encouraged by his experiences.

Mike enjoyed his foray into this quiet space of the library. He had never been a great reader and fancied trying something different. He found a poetry book and enjoyed some of the language he found. He imagined the scenes, finding himself led on a lovely journey. He found words and phrases that really resonated with him; the cry of the seal that 'restrings the wind',[71] the comparison of our gaze being 'submarine' so as our eyes look upward they 'see the light that fractures through unquiet water'.[72] He found himself writing out the odd verse to read over, to let it speak to him and to enjoy the sounds and pictures. It was amazing to find some poems that seemed to sum up his situation.

---

71. From Susan Skinner, 'The Unknown Seal' in *Out of Nowhere* (Searle Publishing, 2010).
72. From T. S. Eliot, 'Choruses from The Rock' in *Collected Poems, 1909-1935* (Faber & Faber, 1942).

The Listening Room

Exploring our story and the importance of being heard

'The most basic of all human needs is the need to understand and be understood. The best way to understand people is to listen to them.'

Dr Ralph Nichols [73]

> This is a cosy room in the retreat centre, with two comfortable armchairs and a small table holding a clock, a box of tissues and glasses of water. This is where Karen listens to people telling their stories, hearing their joys and sorrows and helping them to explore their reactions and relationships.

Dan was having a difficult but interesting experience in hospital. He was going through treatment for cancer of the throat at the tender age of 24. He had suffered the removal of a tumour from his throat three weeks previously and was having further chemotherapy. The side room cut him off from watching any action in the ward

---

73. Dr Ralph Nichols, known as the 'father of the field of listening': http://www.listen.org/Legend.

which added to the boredom of having little energy. The fact that he couldn't speak was also bringing frustrations. His mother often visited but she spent her time being distraught and fidgety and he found his best defence was to shut his eyes as it was too distressing trying to communicate with her. He had a few friends who visited but there were two other visitors who intrigued him. The first was an elderly man who had wandered into his side room a few days before. Dan considered ringing for the nurse as this pyjama-clad man was obviously not meant to be in his room. However, the man had plonked himself down in the chair and continued to speak. He also was bored and sorrowful. As he started sharing about his wife having died recently, Dan didn't have the heart to get someone to remove him. He realised that the fact he couldn't speak was actually encouraging this man, Tom, to continue his story. After a short time though, Tom just got up and went out. Since then he had come in each day to continue his story. Dan felt that the least he could do was to look vaguely interested as it seemed to be cheering him up. Dan also realised that hearing Tom's story was a comfort to himself as well; he didn't feel so alone in his own suffering.

The other visitor who gave him cause to reflect was the chaplain who had popped in one day. When the chaplain realised Dan couldn't speak, he asked if he would like him to sit with him. Dan had found this strangely comforting. There was something about having someone just sit with him, in the situation he was in, that gave him a sense of peace. He felt a connection to this man who now came in each day for a few minutes. At first he really wanted to tell him his story – there was such a lot going on for him, but he found that in this peaceful sitting his story didn't seem so important and, besides, he had already gone over what he might tell this chaplain if he had a voice. These two visitors had given him thoughts about the different interactions that were helpful to him at this really hard time in his life.

It is such a gift to be really heard, to have someone's undivided attention listening to our story. Many of the people we converse with form opinions on what we are saying. They have their own agenda and want to add their part to what is being said. Dan had an interesting experience precisely because he couldn't bring in his own agenda. This room is about really being listened to in an attentive way that means we are heard and validated and accepted for who we are. It is about listening to ourselves, being listened to by God and by others who are trained to listen.

The last few rooms have included ways of connecting to our inner world, where there is the core of ourselves and an inner divine. The everyday nature of our inner journey could be pictured as a flowing river, with what is brought into our lives each day influencing the flow and turbulence of the river. There may be calm times where we drift from one point to another, other times where we come across obstacles and are more challenged, and moments that are more like white water rafting where we get thrown around. With each connection into this river of events, circumstances, emotions and challenges, our responses influence how we navigate. Our beliefs and faith, our reactions and reflections, all influence the way we tackle the everyday flow. The past rooms have included ways of noting our responses and ways of listening to this inner world so we can feel what is happening to our river. This room continues this search for connecting to the path of life by consolidating our story and using others to hear this story. This can enable a way of seeing the course of our river and what is happening in our lives, and to think through our actions, feelings and responses. This room also addresses the suffering that comes into our lives, when our river is most turbulent, as it is when we are suffering that we need the most understanding. The store cupboard will continue this theme.

Though gifted friends can be invaluable in listening and supporting our journeys, they may still be influenced by their own agenda and may have difficulty listening without judgement. This room highlights the benefits of going to someone trained in the art of listening. Dan needed someone who could be empathetic to his situation and the chaplain, with his training, was able to give him what he needed through silence. Talking to someone not involved in our lives means that we emphasise things that we might not talk through with a close friend, as we presume what they may know. Ideally, the trained listener should be a qualified counsellor or spiritual director. Both should have the same skills of reflection and enabling exploration of the journey, with the spiritual director also incorporating discernment of faith within the journey, hearing the perspective of the divine. If we are to share our story it is important to have someone able to cope with the contents of our story and our emotions in a professional way. If we have more immediate problems and difficulties, then a trained counsellor may be suitable. If we would like to explore our journey in relation to the divine, it would be good to find a spiritual director to accompany us. This chapter is an encouragement for ongoing support for our journey, rather than for a few days when we go on retreat. There are many different styles of training for counsellors and spiritual directors and each will have their specialism, so some careful research may need to be done before the right person is found. Some helpful websites and addresses are included at the end of the book.

The confidentiality of this listening room can enable the exploration of the different aspects of the course of our river. The listener can help us to explore the different flows of our river – in present-day as well as past circumstances – and to note the significance of how we respond. The initial sharing of our story can be interesting for ourselves to actually hear what parts we want to share and which bits we miss out. The listener will be reflecting and helping us to hear what we are saying. They will be helping us to dig around what we say, finding further insight. They will note our body language and emphasise some of the bits we were not aware we said and help us develop tools to aid our own listening and observation. It can be an enlightening and fascinating process. (See *Exercise 18.*)

These listening sessions may open up areas of our lives that need some exploration. This is a room where there is a chance to explore what is taking us outside our comfort zone, but the method of actually going through this will also stretch that zone. I often compared my own counselling at a time of distress in my life to the pain of lancing a boil! It was hard but necessary for my healing. Wounds need exploring and excavation, for left alone they might go septic. This is not an easy space at times; exploring may mean entering into dark areas within and courage is required.

The everyday humdrum of life can have the same difficulties of navigation as can major life changes. Boredom can create as many issues as anxiety. Freud proposed that the most disquieting experiences we face are not those that are entirely unfamiliar but moments when the familiar and the unfamiliar meet.[74] We can suffer when we are outside our comfort zone and when

---

74. See Sigmund Freud, *The "Uncanny"* (1919) (available at http://web.mit.edu/ allanmc/www/freud1.pdf).

we do not feel in control. We may experience this lack of control in many aspects of our lives: in physical distress, mental anxieties, emotional frustrations and pain, spiritual grief or past traumas. When there is one aspect of our life that changes – a loved one is suffering, there is pressure in our work, our body is going through the menopause, for example – then it often throws the flow of the river, affecting the whole of our life. Not feeling in control can make us feel stressed and powerless and many of the physical illnesses that the body succumbs to, such as colds and sore throats, happen when we are feeling helpless and hopeless. It often depends on our expectations as to how stressed and powerless we feel. It is easier to manage our lives if we accept that life can be unfair and difficult, often leading to chaotic feelings. If we can learn to tolerate short-term discomfort, perhaps even accepting that what comes into our lives could be a way of developing ourselves and finding more about our depths and faith, then suffering can be a way to define and mould us.

There are ways we can develop our own listening to ourselves and experience the way God can listen to us. This can help us to be more aware of our river and circumstances and enhance what we bring into the presence of a trained listener. When we go through chaos and suffering, much more stress will be brought into our lives but there is still a way to listen to ourselves through this. I had a dream where I was trying to start a car by turning my key into a handful of slimy, sloppy entrails. I had an urge to drive as the previous driver made me feel unsafe. However, I became frustrated with this way of starting the car, having to clean the key and ask for assistance. This dream was something to do with me wanting control and trying to find the 'key' to getting this control in ways that were not working. Further thoughts on the dream showed that the messy guts needed to just be sat with, held out, and I had the ridiculous thought of frying them to make a nutritious and more solid form! Suffering is messy, gutty, emotional and bloody, with no easy answers. What is going on in the emotions is not something that the logical mind can figure out. It needs to be sat with, listened to and brought into God's presence. An anonymous writer once stated: 'Suffering is not a question that demands an answer, not a problem that demands a solution; it is a mystery which demands a presence.' [75] Sitting with the guttiness allows some sort of acceptance, a way of being able to acknowledge the mess and chaos that is around. Then there is a chance to observe, maybe noting the feelings evoked of having someone else driving the car and not being in control.

This sitting with our mess can also allow us to be really listened to by God. It can be hard to sit with our mess in the presence of God and this puts many people off sitting in silence, even though the word 'listen' contains

---

75. Anonymous, quoted in Michael Baughen, *The one big question – the God of love in a world of suffering* (CWR, 2010), p.19.

the same letters as the word 'silent'! It is in this silent space that a pathway can often be found through distress and we can feel heard by a more intimate source than a trained listener. Thomas Keating notes that in this silence there is space to perceive the damage done in childhood or what we have done to ourselves. He compares this sitting with God to an archaeological dig where the Spirit explores our history. As we sit with God, different layers of ourselves get revealed, giving new insights. He goes on to say that we need this time to evacuate our emotional junk. We need a good vomit at times! Keating's suggestion is to cultivate a friendly attitude to this junk so we can acknowledge it and wave it goodbye, maybe with the help of a trained listener. My thought of frying the guts from my dream made me smile, a way of using them for humour, rather than concern. Keating also states that the benefits of this contemplative praying include receiving wisdom, understanding and knowledge.[76] I saw an interview recently with a nun who was talking about her own way of self-analysis, finding that the contemplative life of silence enabled her to find out much about herself as well as her faith. Asked if she had thought of therapy to gain the same sense of self, she answered that contemplation was a lot cheaper! But then she was in a very supportive environment! When we enter this listening room we need to consider listening

---

76. Thomas Keating, *The Better Part*.

to ourselves and the time we spend with God, as well as the benefits of a trained listener, to determine what is the best course of action for our needs.

This way of contemplation through our suffering links in with the 'Examen' introduced in the personal room. Taking some time at the end of the day to notice, in the silence and stillness, what has been good or where there has been joy, beauty or love, can help us to notice the smaller things going on in life during the bigness of the chaos. One woman shared on a course I was on that the Examen got her through depression. It is easy to get overwhelmed with suffering and the Examen helps us to see the bigger picture around and also the day-to-day little things where there has been opportunity to be blessed and strengthened. To notice and be encouraged by the smallness – acts of kindness, funny phrases heard on television, a beautiful flower seen in the garden, a smile, a gesture, a good memory – can all highlight ways in which we are being touched and blessed whilst seeking some answers to life.

Isaac Penington, a seventeenth-century Quaker, wrote a letter about using the small things to reveal our journey:

> Do not look for such great matters to begin with; but be content to be a child, and let the Father proportion out daily to thee what light, what power, what exercises, what fears, what troubles he

sees fit for thee . . . Thou must join in with the beginnings of life, and be exercised with the day of small things, before thou meet with the great things, wherein is the clearness and satisfaction of the soul.

He goes on to say that our journey begins at the start of the day where there is little light and where the detection of good and evil is not very clear. 'Yet there must the traveller begin and travel; and in his faithful travels . . . the light will break in upon him more and more.' [77] There is a sense of the long, slow travelling through life in this quote. Being aware of the different paths of dark and light takes discernment through reflection and learning through the everyday life we lead. Healing in our suffering can often be gradual as there are sometimes many aspects to the suffering that need addressing. Our relationships, our beliefs and attitudes, our lifestyle may all need to be challenged through the chaos and all this needs that slowness of step-by-step journeying.

As we journey through life, we find the different aspects of ourselves. Our inner mosaic that we started to explore in the dining room and lounge can continue to be explored through this listening room. As we listen to ourselves and sit with God and talk through our story, we find the pieces of ourselves that make us who we are. We might hear from a part of us that sounds

---

77. Britain Yearly Meeting, *Quaker Faith and Practice* – http://qfp.quaker.org. uk/passage/19-43/.

particularly wise, for instance, or that sounds like our inner child wanting its say. As we listen and talk we explore many aspects of our personality. The more we find out about ourselves, the more we might explore the aspects of ourselves as being reflected in the God in whom we believe. Suffering takes us to different areas within ourselves where we often find other pieces of ourselves and hence find other aspects of God. (See *Exercise 19*.)

It is easy to get disorientated, stuck in an eddy or lost in our lives and the help of a trained listener to journey alongside us in a one-to-one setting can be valuable in exploring meanings and emotions of what is going on. Talking our story through helps us to hear the parts of the chaos. Like a pile of different coloured threads, we start to draw out one thread at a time, clarifying the construction of our mess. These threads once recognised can explain parts of our lives, and we can choose either to discard them or use them to construct a better path to our life. This can have many benefits; once thoughts have been expressed, there is a chance that they can be looked at from different aspects. What has happened in the past cannot be changed, but sometimes more insight and understanding can lead to a different way of responding, including exploring the difficulties of forgiveness and compassion. Talking through our story can also help us learn ways of surviving the rougher waters, of being able to self-analyse and learn techniques to tackle the different environments in our lives. I recollect one person saying that she shared her sense of drowning with her spiritual director, who replied that perhaps they needed to look at learning to breathe underwater. Often creative ways can come forth and skills seen that can enable change and are valuable when reflecting and decision-making.

Finding meaning and purpose to our lives are essential aspects to coming into this room. Viktor Frankl discovered much about what gives meaning to our lives through his experiences at the horrendous Auschwitz camp. He noticed that the sort of prisoner each person became was the result of an inner decision and not the result of camp influences alone. He saw that the way people bore their suffering was a genuine inner achievement and it was this spiritual freedom that made life meaningful and purposeful. His time in this suffering gave him a unique insight into what human potential achieves. From this Viktor concluded that life is meaningful under any circumstances as human potential allows for the best, including being able to turn suffering into a human achievement and accomplishment. The logotherapy he founded after surviving Auschwitz helped people to find a meaning and purpose to their lives.[78] Talking through our stories can be a way of noting what our gifts are and how we tackle situations. Suffering can help define and mould us as well as highlight how we cope and connect to the path of life.

---

78. Viktor E. Frankl. *Man's Search for Meaning.*

Finding symbols or images relating to our journey can really help to speak of what we are going through. Words such as 'river', 'cave', 'abyss', 'drowning', 'carrying the cross' and 'desert' can all give us images that can be developed and talked through. Job was someone we read about in the Old Testament who also had incredible suffering and he brought to mind the image of a miner chipping away at the rock in the darkness underground to explore the answers to his suffering. As he toils, he uncovers treasures found deep within – wisdom in his ordeal – that would not have been found without the searching.[79] Describing life through the image can help us understand why we feel that way and how it is impacting the rest of life. Emotions need to be noted as they can bring valuable meaning to what is going on, as well as adding to the picture. If we feel like someone in a dark cavern, for instance, then that may make sense of why so many things are difficult at this time. We can then be helped to look at what is needed in this cavern, what is required to survive and what comfort and relationships may be helpful. Highlighting what is not helpful in this environment, – things revealed that need to change or be released – can sometimes be seen more clearly through the image. If God feels distant, then taking the metaphor into consideration can help us find other ways to connect to God. How would we connect to God in a dark cavern?

79. See Job Chapter 28.

The usual ways of prayer may need to change and taking the image to God in a quiet space can sometimes reveal other aspects of how to live life. What to read may also be clearer, as there may be parts of the Bible and other spiritual and secular books that will help us to understand this place.

So what were some of the ways that Job used to find his treasures in his deep darkness? He did a lot of searching, throwing questions out to God, expounding on his condition and venting his emotions and predicament to friends. Questioning ourselves and God can be helpful for exploration. I often encourage people to note the tools they might need to explore their environment; what ways of thinking, observing, noting things down might help to find the wisdom of the journey. (See *Exercise 20*.)

Job threw himself fully into exploring what was going on; he did not try to forget it and think about other things. He sat with his suffering and explored the environment he was in. It is much easier to run away from our problems, to try and cover them up or to keep asking God to take them away. Fixing time with a trained listener is acknowledging the responsibility for managing our own lives. Taking time to explore our pain is loving and valuing ourselves and allowing another's respect and love.

In the difficult environments in which we find ourselves we can often feel cut off from the presence of God. This can cause additional problems. So it is important in this listening room to have space to explore the God we were following when all was going well. There may be an image of the divine or beliefs that are hindering us from finding that presence in this different environment. If the divine does not change, then what is happening with the way we relate in different seasons of life? It might mean that in this more challenging environment our vision of God can be explored and different aspects of God found in the darkness, that we have not encountered previously. Faith can sometimes have more growth in the dark, when we are questioning and reflecting. Our image of God might expand and include one that links with the compassionate and loving voice within, a voice that sheds wisdom and kernels of treasure into the chaos. Job concludes that we have a choice to accept both the good parts of life and the difficulties. 'When God sends us something good, we welcome it. How can we complain when he sends us trouble?' (Job 2:10, *Good News Bible*).

Let us go back to Gillian, whom we met in the library, and see what happened when she came into the listening space and had spiritual direction for some time with me. During her regular sessions there were various aspects of her story that were explored: her upbringing, especially her critical father, her faith and her present difficulties. We took some time to explore her self-image and to find a language where there was opportunity for exploration of the divine. Her image of God was very much connected to her critical father, an image which was also a deeply engrained concept as she used that critical voice so much on herself.

How someone views themself, their self-image, is an important consideration in this listening room. Self-image will be hugely influenced by parenting, security, nurture, love and environment in our childhood. All these different manifestations will affect how a relationship is formed with God. The psychiatrist Gerald May says that one's image of self is no more real than one's image of God. 'The image we have of ourselves – one component of "identity" – deeply affects how we meet the world and the attitudes with which we encounter images of God . . . We are at core endlessly mysterious, and our self-images are simply expedient symbols of who we really are. This is, of course, also true for our images of God.'[80] Who we imagine ourselves and God to be are just symbols of the underlying mystery of our identity, symbols that are necessary for forming our thoughts, but that need to be reviewed for their truth. May goes on to say that the contemplative experience makes it obvious that the 'real' meeting is quite different. This is where the mystery of the person finds a grounding in the eternal mystery of the Creator of all mysteries and where we connect to being made in the image of God.

Finding the language to express mystery is difficult as it is often a sensory experience that words have difficulty describing. As a spiritual director I try and help people

80. Gerald May, *Care of Mind, Care of Spirit*, p.66.

to articulate these meeting experiences. If we can catch a flavour of these deep connections with God – perhaps as an image, a word, a feeling or a presence – then this can really help with feeling more connected to ourselves and to God. We might feel moved at a sunrise, have a fleeting image that makes us think, feel a sense of being held or of companionship, or a sense of calm when praying or meditating, for example. Once we have the taste of God, it is easier to grasp hold of how it affected us and how it could happen again. 'The man who can articulate the movements of his inner life, who can give names to his varied experiences, need no longer be a victim of himself, but is able slowly and consistently to remove the obstacles that prevent the spirit entering.'[81]

With Gillian we found a way of relating that explored other concepts of the divine, rather than using words that hindered (such as God and Father). She found using her imagination was a good tool in her exploration as she imagined a picture of her situation. This included a big black cloud that seemed to be between herself and the divine. She contemplated what might be behind this cloud, to wonder at a bigger Presence. At another time she had an image of a dark wood where she found herself wandering into a clearing where she felt the warming effects of the sun. This helped her to explore sensations that linked her to the divine. Having to make decisions

---

81. Henri Nouwen, *The Wounded Healer* (Doubleday, 1990), p.38.

on a way of change in her life was aided by connecting to a Presence who was not part of the criticism in her life, a Spirit that might offer her support, guidance and love. This went alongside her exploration of observing the way her mind worked. She explored her own thinking patterns and observed the impact of those thoughts. She noted the reactions that had affected her – for instance, there may have been a text that wasn't clear or a comment in a conversation that was easily misinterpreted – and she noted how her thoughts would set off a pattern of negativity and anxiety. These would often escalate and link into other worrying thoughts. She talked through an image of this. It was like a snowball that started off at the top of the mountain with just a small worry forming it, then getting bigger as it escalated down the mountain with more negative thoughts. It would crash at the bottom into a dark pit, a place where escape was difficult and where God seemed absent. Gillian appreciated that this could change and talked through a different scenario. She imagined a rock on the mountain that would smash the snowball, scattering all the pieces.

The anxious thoughts linked into her poor self-image and she realised the thoughts were blocking off her ability to hear her own stronger, positive inner voice. She realised that this positive voice had been getting drowned out, not only by the anxiety, but also by the critical voice within her. Hearing from a place within, where she found encouragement and wisdom, was enlightening and she realised that this was the place where the divine was speaking to her and leading her. The rock on the mountain that smashed the snowball was a solid connection to the divine – a place where her anxieties could be dispersed. It was difficult to trust this place but she noted that this would need her attention and time. Getting this time for her reflections was often difficult but she realised the benefits of sitting quietly, giving herself an opportunity to listen, as well as reading some helpful books.

Being heard in an attentive, non-judgemental way is a valuable experience that can also help us to find our own individual voice, the voice that belongs to our True Self. It is finding that strong inner voice that is often drowned out through stress, distrust, lack of self-esteem and confidence. As explored in the library, there is sometimes a judgemental, critical voice that drowns out our true voice, as well as voices that we have heard in the past that come to ambush the voice of compassion, wisdom and love that we have within. Ruby Wax, who now does a lot for mental health having suffered herself, suggests that we need to realise that our inner critical voice cannot be silenced completely. There will always be an 'internal nag' within us and, once we have accepted this, it is easier to keep negative thoughts in perspective.[82] Having sessions with the listener can help us find and trust a truer voice,

---

82. From *The Week*, July 2013.

an intuitive voice. It can help the victim side of a person to become a survivor and be more assertive.

Talking through our story can bring a way of being able to hear our own strengths and gifts, hearing how we are tackling life now and also how we coped with past events. Our past wounds leave a scar, and, if we allow it, these scars can teach us about our strengths and how we made it through. A couple of questions I sometimes ask in spiritual direction are: 'What are you learning or acquiring now, through this situation?' and 'What might it be drawing you to?' With my own illness it interested me that before I went through a long period of suffering I was a very logical person, having a lot going on in my head. The chronic illness I suffered meant I couldn't concentrate, so I developed other parts of myself that have really made me feel more whole and balanced. The out-of-control places in our lives take us into an alien land where values and beliefs are challenged. My own exploring meant I could understand different points of view and be less prejudiced and more open to other ways. Our scars and our wounds show us about our identity and can be opportunities for letting in light to our darkness. Jesus mentioned that we all have the light of life within us, and resting in these dark places can get that seed of that life to grow up into the light and show us our true shape.

On one retreat I ran for chronically ill people I encouraged them to think through their gifts and strengths. We looked at the parable of the talents, in which we are told of a man who entrusted his property to three servants, giving them each a different proportion. Many people going through long-term problems will tend to relate to the servant who was given the least and was unable to do anything with this wealth, apart from hide it away. We spent some time looking at all that was needed to go through a long-term illness. We came up with a full page on the flip chart ranging from patience, strength, courage, pacing, being insightful, to managing others' expectations and many others. These all linked into the gifts of each person and there was a realisation that perhaps they had been given many strengths to cope with life, qualities that had been developed through their trials. The story finishes with the lovely words of the master – 'Well done, good and faithful servant! . . . Come and share your master's happiness!' (Matthew 25:21) – which needed to be heard.

Jesus demonstrated ways to embrace pain. He told his disciples that to follow him they must take up their cross, to accept the suffering on the way and be prepared to make themselves vulnerable. He was very passive in the last few days of his life, experiencing the cruelty of others. Our cross represents the lack of control times that we go through, the suffering times – when there is often pain, isolation and anguish. We are much more use to others if we have learnt how to bear our own cross. St Paul stated about his suffering that 'If we suffer, it is for your help and salvation; if we are helped, then you too are helped and given the strength to endure with patience the same sufferings that we also endure' (2 Corinthians 1:6, Good News Bible). Whatever came on his path, Paul saw as developing his own strength and connecting more to Christ's sufferings, with the outcome of being able to help others in a better way. I feel my own vulnerability and being in touch with my own cross means that I am less likely to be in a position of giving advice, as I know how difficult suffering can be, with no easy answers. The listening room is a good place to explore our own crosses and also the effect of that vulnerability.

It is in the vulnerable, suffering state that a sense of protection and security is needed. There are many images in the Bible that remind us of the nurture, protection and care that God offers: God as a shield, as a strong tower and covering us with his robe of righteousness, for instance. Psalm 91 expresses some of these thoughts:

> He will cover you with his feathers.
> He will shelter you with his wings.
> His faithful promises are your armour and
> protection . . .
> If you make the Lord your refuge,
> if you make the Most High your shelter,
> no evil will conquer you . . .
> The Lord says, 'I will rescue those who love me.
> I will protect those who trust in my name.

When they call on me, I will answer;
I will be with them in trouble.
I will rescue and honour them.'
Psalm 91:4, 9-10, 14-15 (New Living Translation)

It is our true self that God promises to protect; this is the core of ourselves that is often exposed through suffering and through the listening room. This sacred part, which is so connected to our cross, is what God contains and shelters and it is this aspect that I encourage others to find in this listening room.

Our sufferings often come from similar roots within, so we may recognise others' suffering and get a sense of not being so alone in our own journey. Every person has a story that will be enhanced and developed through listening, and going through the listening room will show us how helpful it is to be understood so we can then be better assistants to others.

For Consideration

- What do I notice when I observe my circumstance?
- What is it like for me to sit and be listened to by God?
- How do I cope with suffering?
- Is there someone I need in my life to listen to my story?

Mike's Story

Mike was appreciating his sessions with Karen; they made him feel that he was not so alone. Sharing parts of his story and being asked to think through his talents was a novel experience, and something that was helping him form a picture of himself. Using his hands to model clay in the art room had been something he had particularly appreciated and he was still amazed by what came out of that clay. Karen helped him to talk through this experience and he was able to voice his concerns about his health and what that now entailed in his life.

Just talking about this very different life he was now leading felt a relief. It challenged him when Karen asked if he had an image of his life at present. A picture of a desert came to mind and he found himself describing the bleak, dusty surroundings and his aloneness. Karen asked him where the sense of the divine might be in this image and he found himself imagining a small hut he could see on his right. When he ventured inside, it was a sheltered empty space but one that reminded him of his times in the chapel. He knew these times of silence in his life were somehow making him feel more peaceful and were bringing up thoughts about himself, so he recognised they were an important aspect in this desert environment. He used this desert image to sit with; it made him think about what he needed to cope in this environment, such as an understanding friend and time to sort out his life. Karen also encouraged him to describe the God connected to this sheltered hut in his desert and to think about this relationship.

Vanessa's Story

Vanessa was surprised at how she appreciated telling her story to Karen. She had not been to a trained listener before and found expressing the anxiety in her life, and exploring the roots of this, an interesting experience to observe. It was just so lovely to get some understanding. She found that the creative ways she was experiencing in the retreat also added to her observation. The colours expressed in the art room were a visual link to her emotions and she could feel a sense of change inside her when bringing in the divine. Observing her mind had been another enlightening exercise for her and she was keen to talk through what she had found.

Karen listened to her as she tried to explain how her mind worked in various instances – when she was anxious and when she felt low. She talked to Karen about more space that she wanted in her mind and how this might be created.

In one session Vanessa found herself saying something that sounded particularly wise. Karen encouraged her to note the voice of this wisdom. Vanessa developed an image of a wise person within her – it was a comfortable-looking woman who was practical and full of common sense. Karen encouraged her to use her imagination to visit this woman and Vanessa enjoyed visiting her in a cottage in a wood where they would sit down with home-baked scones and Vanessa would tell her of a problem or thought and would listen to what this wise woman would say to her. She found it really enlightening to find this wise person within and was excited to realise that it also reflected an aspect of God within her.

The Store Cupboard

Noticing the place of difficult emotions, unmet needs and suffering in our lives

This being human is a guest house.
Every morning a new arrival.

A joy, a depression, a meanness,
some momentary awareness comes
as an unexpected visitor.

Welcome and entertain them all!

From The Guest House by Jelaluddin Rumi (1207-73) [83]

> This is a large cupboard under the stairs in the retreat house. It has a light that shines onto the useful items at the front – gadgets that assist with keeping the house maintained. Behind these is a dark cluttered mess where unwanted and misplaced articles or items that have no other home have collected.

83. Coleman Barks (trans.), 'The Guest House' in *Rumi: Selected Poems* (Penguin Classics, 2004).

One holiday I visited a National Trust property that had been kept in its Victorian state. It was a very personal house, the owner having kept many items that highlighted the way of living in that era. In the most intimate room of the house – the bedroom – there was an animated guide, who told the story of the couple who had dreamt and dressed in this room. I was getting restless, having seen much history by this stage, but then the guide turned to the wardrobe. He paused for dramatic effect and then opened the carved wooden door. What was revealed came as a complete surprise to me and I found myself standing there really moved. There in front of us were two stunning dresses from the 1890s. The intricate lace on beautiful silk was quite breathtaking. The relatives who had lived in the house in later years had used them as dressing-up clothes before they were preserved! I reflected later as to why I felt so moved – what was being revealed was someone's personal wardrobe, items treasured by someone. It was something about the opening of the wardrobe, of the not-knowing to the revealing. It spoke to me of the surprises in life, the way the emotions can be stirred at unexpected moments.

There are many influences that help us to connect with the path of life and many that turn us down that difficult path that opposes the way to life. This section will cover some of the difficulties we may come across that pull us away from a meaningful, life-giving journey. The store cupboard represents some of the hidden obstacles that may be hindering our journey for light and life. There are so many issues, habits, beliefs and emotions that can pull us away from this path. This chapter will not be covering separate issues; rather, it will confront how we acknowledge those dark areas within and how we can go about cleaning out some of the dusty and ill-fitting pieces that we no longer need.

This store cupboard chapter follows the listening space as it is often in this space that the store cupboard is approached. Sitting quietly in God's presence can make us aware of some of the clutter in our lives and bring up past memories for insight. Speaking to a counsellor or spiritual director can also access this cupboard, finding parts of ourselves that have been forgotten or unloved. So the initial step of accessing this cupboard is to acknowledge that we all have needy areas within. We all have a place of storage full of fears, difficult memories and unmet needs. To include this place in our retreat is important as its exploration will access items that will be stopping our growth and freedom and teach us much about ourselves.

When beginning this exploration it is important to note the advantages of being in the observer position; opening the door of the cupboard and having a rummage around in the dark may just induce a huge sense of anxiety. (See *Exercise 21*.) This store cupboard is deep inside our internal world, and the position of the observer is outside the cupboard, just noting what it can see and feel. The observer is also noting the reactions in the body, mind, spirit and emotions so that sensitive issues can be tackled in a way that is paced and manageable and does not overwhelm. There is a distanced and non-judgemental insight from ourselves as the observer, listening to the wisdom and insight of the divine. I find the image of having my feet on solid rock a helpful connection to God's presence. This is a stance that reminds me of the solid, unchanging, loving, everlasting presence of God. Being rooted in this love brings a strength to cope with the insights of the cupboard, whether they be lovely surprises or unwelcome guests. Others find that if they keep in mind the sense of Jesus next to them this can also give them courage and help their awareness. Solomon adds his own advice:

> My son, do not let wisdom and understanding out
> of your sight,
> preserve sound judgment and discretion;
> they will be life for you,
> an ornament to grace your neck.
> Then you will go on your way in safety,
> and your foot will not stumble.
> When you lie down, you will not be afraid;
> when you lie down, your sleep will be sweet.
> Have no fear of sudden disaster
> or of the ruin that overtakes the wicked,

for the Lord will be at your side
and will keep your foot from being snared.

Proverbs 3:21-26

Jesus had 40 days in the desert to reflect on his life and ministry and must have had to face his inner demons in these difficult days. During this time his reliance and communication with God must have been vital. The knowledge that he was loved by his Father would have given him inner security to be able to face the difficult parts of his humanity and what was being asked of him. St Luke mentions that Jesus was filled with the power of the Spirit as he came back from the desert, and it is something about Jesus' exploring of his inner depths that facilitated this infilling and enabled him to help others with their difficulties and enter into their depths. His actions flowed from this Spirit and his interior communication with God. Finding a personal, intimate God at our core, someone who loves and values us and wants the best for us, can help us to have some stability and wisdom when peering into our cupboard. What is found becomes a way of understanding who we really are; our weaknesses and issues become areas of learning.

The Interior Castle by St Teresa of Avila is a guide for spiritual development through service and prayer, marking seven stages of faith to connect to God at the centre of the castle.[84] St Teresa stresses that the spiritual

---

84. St Teresa of Avila, *The Interior Castle* (Doubleday, 1961).

life is about the pursuit of God, not the pursuit of yourself, saying that if the object of your inner journey becomes only yourself then you may suffer discontent, depression or anxiety because you are imploding from attention to your fears as opposed to your release from them. So looking into the store cupboard is a way of looking inward in order to connect outward. It is focusing on ourselves as a healthy position of care and value. It is not a position of selfishness or feeling unworthy. The spiritual path is about opening the way, clearing any obstacles so that God's light and enlightenment can reach these dark places and illuminate them.

St Teresa encourages working with the soul or our true self to examine the nature of the psyche and emotions, this being done through prayer. She suggests the first stage of prayer is getting to know yourself which requires a gathering together of parts of your spirit that you have neglected, forgotten or attached to others. To help in this discovery, she proposes conversation with your soul, a way of conversational prayer to gain the courage to have an open exchange with God, trying to hear this voice. To begin the conversation, a prayer is said, followed by a time for quiet and listening, as if you are establishing the practice of dialogue. You pray and listen, pray and listen and go into silence. The dialogues with your soul may reveal many emotions and insights but you are not doing this to invite self-pity but to find the hidden value. Caroline Myss comments on this way of conversational prayer: 'You're mining these chunks of raw emotion so you can find the value hidden within them. Sit with each discovery until you can see through the raw ore to the gold or jewel it holds. At every opportunity choose fearlessness: do not run from whatever you discover, whether you find pain or untapped talent. Be fearless. Fearlessness is bliss.'[85] Finding a dialogue through the issues that are being brought up in the silence of prayer can help us to analyse the contents of the cupboard. I find that writing about these findings in my journal in one colour pen, then changing the colour of the pen to write what I perceive God to be saying into the findings can be very enlightening.

A useful insight can be gained when exploring store cupboard issues by finding out more about our personality type. Both the Myers-Briggs Type Indicator (MBTI) personality test and the Enneagram highlight useful information about our behaviour – what issues we might be prone to and where our problem areas may be. The MBTI is based on Jung's psychological types and covers 16 different areas. The Enneagram groups individuals into nine areas. Oscar Ichazo taught the Enneagram from the 1960s, using components from mystical Judaism, Christianity, Islam, Taoism, Buddhism, and ancient Greek philosophy. We are all unique, so none of us will fit exactly into any type and these types are

---

85. Caroline Myss, *Entering the Castle: An Inner Path to God and Your Soul* (Simon and Schuster, 2007), p.287.

not definitive and cannot be used to predict or prescribe the future. However, they do help us to understand how we may react to our environment and relationships and why others of different personality types may upset and frustrate us and cope very differently with the contents of their store cupboard.

As we stand before our store cupboard, it is worth noting the various thoughts that might stop the exploration of this inner store. There may be a fear of what will be found or a questioning of the point of looking inward. Whether we have the incentive and discipline to do so may also be mulled over. It is worth listening to these thoughts and taking them into account. There needs to be a sense of incentive into finding a better way for ourselves. We are worth it, and it will benefit our way. We are not responsible for what we have been given in the early stages of our life, but we can make ourselves accountable for what we do with the baggage accumulated from our upbringing. We are each responsible for our cupboard and its junk – no one else will be sorting it out.

So from the outside of the cupboard it is worth noting what is going on in the mind, body, spirit and emotions that might link to debris that has been put to the back of this store. The mind has been discussed in the library but it is worth noting the different voices being heard in the head and where they are leading. What is the voice that sounds the loudest? There is often a battle going on between voices – I can't/I can; shall I/shan't I – one that seems to be freer and one that often wants control and safety. Some say that there is a wounded side of us, needing to be heard. Whatever voices we have going on in our self-talk, it is worth from this observer position noting them and how they are affecting our path of life. There may also be images, past conversations and memories floating around. So this is a noting time to see what in the mind might be putting obstacles in our path.

These times of noting our cupboard also need to be paced. Peering into our cupboard will need to be at a time where we are calm and relaxed and have set some time aside for this purpose. It will be valuable time, as noting the cupboard will help us to create a better space within to sort and sift through issues. If we are in a good inner space then when we are hurt, upset or ignored, we are more prone to act with some patience and understand. If the cupboard is never acknowledged or is in a state of disarray, then we are more likely to react negatively to this pressure. We need to observe with loving patience and lots of nurturing of ourselves. It is important we find that nurturing, loving voice within that will help us sort through what might be in our cupboard. We can all usually think of someone in our lives who has been that loving voice, and linking to what that person might say to us through this time can help us to hear some tenderness. The junk that might be stored within may need firmness and wisdom to understand and deal with, but without compassion towards ourselves we could just become impatient. As the poem at the start of this chapter suggested, we can welcome all that comes to us, seeing our issues as visitors to be entertained. It is also worth noting that the cupboard has a door that can be closed. We have the choice to open and to close the door, to contain our difficult issues and continue with everyday life until the time is right to face these issues.

The following are some thoughts that are worth keeping in mind if we are being particularly hard on ourselves:

- Note that I am a fallible human being and that I can learn from my errors and make amends if need be. This requires admitting responsibility for my actions and having a healthy self-acceptance. I can forgive myself and ask forgiveness from God.

- I need to realise that past actions are based on the situation I was in and the belief I had about that situation. If I am constantly thinking that I should have known then what I know now – and didn't – then I need to know that I have acted in exactly the way I did, given what was in my mind at the time.

- I am not responsible for what goes in other people's lives or the environment. I can only be responsible for myself. I do not have a large amount of control over my environment or other people. I do not have to assume responsibility for other people's happiness.

Then, continuing with the observer position, note what is affecting the state of the body, especially noting feelings and emotions. Emotions are particularly helpful with their messages that can highlight what is going on in our store cupboard. Feelings are involuntary, inner spontaneous reactions to what is happening around us and they have no morality – they just are. Our emotions create physical sensations in our bodies which we can either pay attention to or ignore. It is how we choose to respond to them that leads us to a better or worse outcome. We feel the way that we think, so we need to assume emotional responsibility. If we continually ignore our emotions, they start festering in the store cupboard and can create physical and mental health problems. If they are listened to, perhaps in the quiet stillness of contemplation, they can be noted and their message received. The Examen is especially helpful for listening to our emotions.

Anger is one emotion that is often suppressed in our cupboard. Anger is aroused when we perceive that we are threatened, rejected, put down, ignored or humiliated, and we are often made angry through the actions of others. Anger usually follows hurt, and suppression of anger can lead to sickness and depression, whilst control of anger is a key factor in the solution of many problems, from childhood defiance and marital conflict to mental or physical illness. Freud once likened anger to the smoke in an old-fashioned wood-burning stove, in which the normal avenue for the discharge of the smoke is up the chimney. This is equivalent to how anger can be safely expressed, like punching pillows, shouting into the wind or banging doors. If the normal avenue is blocked, the smoke will leak out of the stove in unintended ways – around the door or through the grates, for example – choking everyone in the room. If all avenues of escape are blocked, the fire goes out and the stove ceases to function. So anger is one emotion, like many others, that it is good to recognise and express in a safe way. There is a difference between righteous and vengeful anger. Jesus shows righteous anger through the action of cleansing the temple (John 2:13-17), and God's righteous anger is aroused when widows and orphans are ill-treated and cry out to God (Exodus 22:22-24). Human anger is harmful when expressed for self-centred motives but is warranted when expressed against real injustice when it can be a motivational force, one that can help lead us forward on our paths. (See *Exercises 22a–c* for ways of handling some of our emotions.)

Guilt and shame can be other strong emotions that affect our journeys. Guilt is experienced when we fail to live up to our moral standard or ethical values, or when we feel we have harmed or injured someone. It can also be an emotion stemming from the belief that one is bad or immoral. Shame can be an awareness of our human limitations. It is experienced when we have revealed an inadequacy or feel inferior to other people – for example, when they have judged us. Shame can also become a debilitating sense of being unlovable, stemming from a belief that one is flawed and so inadequate and inferior to others. We need to note our thoughts in relation to emotions in order to experience what they are doing to us – how they are making us react and behave.

The amygdala is one area in the brain that is influenced by our emotions. Stress and anxiety play an important part in stimulating this area and are major influences in our store cupboards. The amygdala is involved in turning on the stress response, triggering adrenaline which causes cortisol secretion. Higher levels of the hormone cortisol in the blood stream trigger the 'flight or fight' reflex. This adrenaline-fuelled state alerts the body to be ready to run away – helpful when you are in a situation of danger, but not if the body does not actually fight or run, so the adrenaline is left to subside more slowly, leaving the person feeling agitated for a long time. Leading an adrenaline-fuelled life can become addictive but eventually this state reduces the hormone serotonin in the body, less serotonin leading to a lower mood. Adrenaline makes the heart beat faster and the digestive system slow down to allow more blood to be sent to muscles, so if the amygdala continues to be stimulated then the body ends up in a constant stress state where the activity is in the muscles, often causing pain if continuous. Diet can also produce a sense of unease, with stimulants like caffeine and alcohol and too much salt and sugar causing problems with adrenaline surges. This wired state can become a long-term problem leading to a pattern of difficulty sleeping, fatigue, digestive problems and low energy. The immune system will also be weakened so infections are picked up more readily and this state can also fuel anxiety as it makes us more likely to have fearful, negative thoughts and be more jumpy and lacking in concentration. To get out of this stress state the body needs to be brought into a healing state, one where there is mental relaxation, slowing down the fast beta waves to the slower alpha waves, and a way of breathing that is slower and deeper. Finding our inner chapel space, the stillness within, will help us achieve this healing state, as will connecting to the body. Breathing and mindfulness exercises, a brisk walk, some stretches or just mental rest, doing something creative maybe, may assist with lowering adrenaline and helping energy to flow in a more life-giving way.

Anxiety affects people in different ways. Some people are naturally more anxious because of their personality, their upbringing and the way they deal with their thoughts.

I did some work with a young person on the anxious feelings she was experiencing in her gut. Having drawn out these feelings in light and dark colours, shown as complex scribbles on paper, we took various wools and cut different strands to represent the feelings. As she looked at and touched these wools, she was able to consider what they might represent. She thought of a situation during which some of them had been activated. She had been in a shop where the alarms kept going off. She had enjoyed the shopping experience but the alarms had produced some fear. So the strands both of bright excitement and of dark fear were seen. She also recognised the one that represented the unknown. To her this was the most important and needed to go on the top. It was a strand that represented the not-knowing, the uncertainty of what lies around the corner. She knew that only God knew what was going to happen and this was recognised as a hard thought to take on board, especially for a sensitive young person.

Worry and anxiety can be real obstacles to the inner spirit as they keep us connected to our ego and our old ways of thinking and habits. It occurred to me that anxiety is also a vanity, as it means I am hoping for things to go the way I would like, within my comfort zone, and this highlights my lack of trust in a divine way that leads to a better way than mine. I used to get very anxious over travel, timings, getting to places and whether there would be any difficulties along the way. I now try and see the bigger picture and reflect that whatever might occur – missing the train, getting held up by an accident on the motorway, or bad weather, for instance – there is a sense of the alternative and what it might be revealing. Am I able to connect with God through the anxiety of being outside my comfort zone? What do I observe in myself and others through a different way? It is an alternative way of living to recognise God's world and a divine input, rather than the earthly world that requires timings and structure. I now get a sense of 'looking over' events rather than getting stuck in the anxiety within them. Having a good image in my mind, a picture of a positive outcome, or just one that is of beauty and calm, is also a good technique if life is getting fraught.

I found handling worry is also about trusting the decisions I make. If I have organised things in my life, then I need to trust that I have made the right decision at that time and to go along with what is going to happen, rather than fret about the way it will happen. The *Serenity Prayer* is a lovely prayer to have around when worried.

> God grant me the serenity to accept the things
> I cannot change; courage to change the things
> I can; and wisdom to know the difference.
> Living one day at a time; enjoying one moment
> at a time; accepting hardships as the pathway
> to peace. [86]

Letting go of fear and worry is a difficult process, but staying with the here and now, connecting to the senses,

---

86. This is the first section of *The Serenity Prayer* attributed to Reinhold Niebuhr (1892-1971).

moving slowly and appreciating the small things as we go along in life can be helpful. There are also more thoughts in *Exercise 22d.*

There will be many reactions that take us straight into our store cupboard. There will be times when certain sounds, smells, ways people react and memories take us into this cupboard. For example, a person might be reminded of difficult memories every time they hear an ambulance siren. Another may find a difficult past image keeps getting replayed in her mind. A husband might find that every time his wife playfully nibbles his neck he freezes and has a sinking feeling in his stomach. Someone asked me to be a listening ear to help her with her grief over the death of her grandmother. The main problem for her was that there was a particular image that kept re-occurring in her mind of something that happened to her grandmother's body as she was dying. She could not get past this difficult image. She talked through the last hours of her grandmother's death and was able to tell me in detail what had happened. I asked her where God might have been in these last few hours. She became more animated as she talked of the family surrounding her grandmother, of the hymn they sang to her and the amazing way that they were able to let her go at the end. After talking, my friend realised that she had been able to see the bigger picture around for her at that crucial and special time in the last few hours of her grandmother's life. She found that the image no longer had any hold over her. There will be many reactions that we can notice and consider as we take some time to peer into our cupboard. There are some suggestions about ministering to our store cupboard issues in *Exercises 23a–d*.

When we start to peer inside our cupboard it often brings an understanding as to why our life is the way it is and why we react in the way we do. Once I started noting things I found my internal language became more familiar. The dreams I had, the colours I used, the issues that upset me all became clearer and I was able to adapt better. Changing habits is really difficult but if we can see how they are blocking up our cupboards, then we have more incentive to change. There also needs to be a sense of trust that what is found, when going at a slow pace of revelation, is right for us and will be something we can handle – maybe with extra help from someone to share the way.

As the issues are illuminated, acknowledged and listened through to hear God's wisdom, there needs to be a way of releasing and letting go of what we have found in our store cupboard. This process includes shedding the parts of us that are stopping us from linking to the God within. These are the parts that do not feel like the true or real part of us. As we start to link more to God and find out who we really are, we can begin to see the parts that may be masking this new self. They may be masks we have put on to protect ourselves, habits we have formed to make our lives what they are, and ways of reacting so we don't get too emotional. It is whatever is stopping us from feeling joy and spontaneity, and from allowing love into our lives.

Letting go means a detachment from what is found in this cupboard. It is not a cutting off from the contents, but a way of getting back into the observer position with God, so the wisdom from what is found is taken on board and acted upon. This can be a difficult process and there is much self-help that can be obtained, such as that found in the Twelve-Step Programme. The success of Alcoholics Anonymous (AA) has been based on this programme where personal recovery is encouraged through this letting go. These steps are relevant for any issues that we are trying to hang on to and we can substitute our own words where appropriate.

The Twelve Steps based on the experience of the earliest members of AA are as follows (I have added my own suggestions in italics):

1. We admitted we were powerless over alcohol (*substitute other issues*) – that our lives had become unmanageable.
2. Came to believe that a Power greater than ourselves could restore us to sanity.
3. Made a decision to turn our will and our lives over to the care of God as we understood Him.
4. Made a searching and fearless moral inventory of ourselves.

5. Admitted to God, to ourselves and to another human being the exact nature of our wrongs.

6. Were entirely ready to have God remove all these defects of character.

7. Humbly asked Him to remove our shortcomings.

8. Made a list of all persons we had harmed, and became willing to make amends to them all.

9. Made direct amends to such people wherever possible, except when to do so would injure them or others.

10. Continued to take personal inventory and when we were wrong promptly admitted it.

11. Sought through prayer and meditation to improve our conscious contact with God as we understood Him, praying only for knowledge of His will for us and the power to carry that out.

12. Having had a spiritual awakening as the result of these steps, we tried to carry this message to alcoholics (*or relevant others*) and to practice these principles in all our affairs.[87]

These Twelve Steps have helped millions of people out of addictions. Our issues may be different but looking at and noting moral standards, acknowledging a Higher

---

87. http://www.alcoholics-anonymous.org.uk/About-AA/The-12-Steps-of-AA.

Power, (that does not need to be a 'Him') and taking time to pray and meditate to hear God's voice and calling will all help with the process of letting go. When our cupboard issues have led to wrongdoing, then making amends can help process our cupboard. There is also the element of spreading the values of our findings to others. Many find it helpful to identify a small group of people to work with, where each is accountable for their own cupboard issues and shares with the group how they are looking at and coping with these issues.

Connecting to the divine offers a way of cleansing and forgiveness with what is found in our cupboard. The prophet Ezekiel in 593BC was sent to God's people who had been captured by the Babylonians. He gave them the following message from God:

> For I will take you out of the nations; I will gather you from all the countries and bring you back into your own land. I will sprinkle clean water on you, and you will be clean; I will cleanse you from all your impurities and from all your idols. I will give you a new heart and put a new spirit in you; I will remove from you your heart of stone and give you a heart of flesh.And I will put my Spirit in you and move you to follow my decrees and be careful to keep my laws. Then you will live in the land I gave your ancestors; you will be my people, and I will be your God. I will save you from all your uncleanness.

Ezekiel 36:24-29

God offers to cleanse people from inner clutter and give them a tender, responsive heart. This is a heart that is receptive to inspiration from God's inner Spirit. So, as the Twelve Steps mention, there is a process that God offers to remove our defects of character and our shortcomings and through which we may experience cleanliness and purity of heart.

I find using the breath helpful to connect to the cleansing that God offers. I imagine the breath going right through my body and cleaning out any debris in mind, heart or gut that I then breathe out. It is an exercise I sometimes do before seeing the people I work with, so that I clear out my own thoughts to connect with a cleared out space inside me.

Confession of our wrongdoing is part of the process of cleansing. Some of the clutter in our cupboards is to do with acts that we regret or times when we have moved off the path that we know is right for us. In Psalm 32 David describes what happened when he did not acknowledge the things that were polluting him:

> When I kept it all inside,
> my bones turned to powder,
> my words became daylong groans.
>
> The pressure never let up;
> all the juices of my life dried up.

Then I let it all out;
I said, 'I'll make a clean breast of my failures
to God.'

Suddenly the pressure was gone –
my guilt dissolved,
my sin disappeared.'

Psalm 32:3-5 (The Message)

This is about acknowledging that some of the clutter in our cupboard is to do with when we have taken wrong turnings or when we are being pulled off our course. There needs to be some way of shining the light into this area – whether through creative ways of drawing or writing out our confession, confessing out loud to God, to a confidential friend or in the confines of the listening room. Alongside this there needs to be a sense of forgiveness of oneself as well as others, and the hearing and receiving of God's faithful forgiveness.

Cleaning out the cupboard is a humbling process. Like the general housework of toilet cleaning, vacuuming and scrubbing floors these are tasks that not many people recognise or talk about, but they are in fact very necessary to living in the house. The more clutter that is found, the more there will be a realisation of how we need the grace, forgiveness and wisdom of God. This sense of being humble needs to be continually held, in order to keep working through things in the cupboard. We will never be able to completely empty out our cupboard as there will always be issues to work on, but we will have the tools for more efficient cleansing.

As the journey continues and we work through issues in our cupboard our personality will be developing. Paul writes in his letter to the Romans of this change, connecting it to the suffering of dealing with our cupboard findings: 'we know that suffering produces perseverance; perseverance, character; and character, hope' (Romans 5:3-4). There will be something about the process of shining a light into our cupboard that will be moulding us into our true character. There will be a noticing of some of the ways we have been following and our motivations for doing so. We may be following a desire for pleasure, or a way to avoid pain for instance, or want to be secure or successful. As the spiritual journey continues, some of these attachments will be released as the cupboard is confronted. This might cause other items to be placed in the cupboard as the ego or the old self will note this as an underlying threat, still wanting to follow the old way of living. This could appear as a decrease in confidence and, with change of thoughts and ways of being, there may be disorientation as to how to live now. So getting rid of attachments can cause distress and there may also be an underlying sadness linked to the grieving process of letting go of these old ways; what is turned out and let go of in the cupboard will somewhere need to be mourned.

> Spiritual growth demands much that we are
> unwilling to give. It threatens to loosen our
> cherished attachments, to change or even dissolve
> our frozen images of ourselves, and to reveal certain
> truths about ourselves that we are loath to admit.
> Further, it asks sacrifices of our time, energy, and
> resources; it demands our very hearts. It should
> not be surprising to find ourselves resisting that
> which we consciously desire.[88]

Life will be changing and there needs to be recognition of this, along with gentle nurture.

The benefits of shining a light into the cupboard will include development of ourselves to be of use to our natural calling rather than getting stuck in a difficult path. 'In a well-furnished kitchen there are not only crystal goblets and silver platters, but waste cans and compost buckets – some containers used to serve fine meals, others to take out the garbage. Become the kind of container God can use to present any and every kind of gift to his guests for their blessing' (2 Timothy 2:20-21, *The Message*). Cleaning out what we can from the cupboard can refine our true calling so that we are more use to ourselves and to our community.

---

88. Gerald May, *Care of Mind, Care of Spirit*, p.24.

For Consideration

- What are my emotions telling me about my store cupboard?
- How would I want to explore some of the issues I might have?
- How could I connect to God through my difficulties?

Vanessa's Story

Vanessa's retreat experience brought a realisation that she needed to get some regular support in her life. She started to meet with a spiritual director and was finding this helpful to explore her general anxiety and to challenge where her faith was going. Talking through her life and her present situation made her realise the differences that were going on around her. Her two teenage daughters were both going through many changes and she realised that she needed to review the way that she mothered them. There was often a lot of tension in the house as one of the girls wanted more freedom to go out with friends, while the other daughter was becoming more withdrawn and resented telling Vanessa much about herself at all. Alongside this, she was not able to spend the time she would have liked with her husband and was missing his support. Her own job was becoming routine and so Vanessa found she was bored and restless.

She put aside some time each week to reflect and continue some of the things the retreat had opened up for her. Sometimes she drew out her emotions, especially when she noted her tension and frustration. This was helping her to look at what was going on inside her and she often found herself developing the colours into further images. She bought herself some watercolour paints and paper and just enjoyed wetting the paper and seeing what happened with the paint. She was fascinated with the process of letting the uncontrolled and random dollops of paint speak to her in their chaos and beauty.

At other times Vanessa reflected on an event in her week, and she did this in her imagination, picturing the event as though on a cinema screen. She really loved this technique as it made her watch herself, alongside whoever was there and whatever was going on, and she could see then, so clearly, why she did what she did and why she was feeling those particular emotions. As had been suggested to her, she then brought in the divine presence to the screen and could sometimes see a shift or change in the scene. Sometimes she brought in a figure representing Jesus and that was always interesting to see what happened next. She appreciated finding a good way for her to reflect and it always led her into a way of talking to God that seemed much more real than what she had been doing before.

Vanessa also gave herself time to identify the things that she enjoyed doing. She found sometimes her husband

and one or both of her daughters joined in with what she was suggesting. Thinking of the occasional fun thing wasn't so difficult when her mind was more relaxed.

Mike's Story

Mike had been coming back to the retreat every few months as he had been finding a regular short stay really helpful in this difficult time of his life. It had taken a lot to persuade himself that this was what he needed as he had initially been reluctant to part with the money, being quite hard up at the time, and he had found it easy to persuade himself that maybe he could sort himself out on his own. However, once he had been a couple of times, he realised that having a nurturing space was actually improving his health and really helping him deal with unemployed life.

Mike was interested to observe his own life, finding it intrigued him to find out what he actually liked and what his body needed. He found it useful to observe his energy levels as fatigue was one of the symptoms of his ill health and he still got confused as to why some days he felt really washed out, whereas other days he felt OK. He realised that when he met with his mother, for instance, or even if he just had a telephone conversation with her, his energies would start to flag and it often made him feel depressed. He knew he would have to work out how to cope with this difficult relationship in his life.

He was also surprised to find that he had many emotions churning around. One day he decided to write a letter to God and found that once he got writing he covered many pages. He blurted out all that had happened to him in the last few months and found himself scrawling in big letters about how angry and hurt he was at his boss. He had a good rant and ended up feeling a bit better about these events. He then took a clean sheet of paper, as instructed by Miles at the retreat, to write down what he thought God might say in reply to this letter. He felt rather foolish as he started on this clean sheet, but decided he was not going to procrastinate but just start writing. This is what he found came from his pen:

'You are my precious child and I have watched you blowing in the wind. I hear your cries, your flurries of feelings, I see your stability and your resilience and patience. I am an emotional God and hurt at the injustices of the world. I weep with the lonely and get angry at insensitivities. Note where you are. It is a difficult stage, a real transition. Connect with me in your deepest self. Let go of your shame and guilt. What will be will be. Hear my song over you; it is a song that has a rhythm to pace yourself to. It is a song of love and strength and one that you will hear through the storms in your life. I love you.'

Mike was overwhelmed by these words that came onto the page. He found them coming from a different source to his own words. These words seemed so open and loving and it led him to a deep gratitude to God.

The Garden

Allowing nature to connect us to the path of life and reflecting on transformation in our lives

'Sometimes since I've been in the garden I've looked up through the trees at the sky and I have had a strange feeling of being happy as if something was pushing and drawing in my chest and making me breathe fast. Magic is always pushing and drawing and making things out of nothing. Everything is made out of Magic; leaves and trees, flowers and birds, badgers and foxes and squirrels and people. So it must be all around us. In this garden – in all the places.'

Francis Hodgson Burnett [89]

> The garden in the retreat is an important space outside of the building. As this is the last space to come to in the retreat, I leave the reader to imagine their own garden that they would like to explore.

---

89. Frances Hodgson Burnett, *The Secret Garden* (1910) – http://www.online-literature.com/burnett/secretgarden/23/.

I write in my study looking out onto a small part of my back garden. One year, out of this seemingly infertile brick-paved area a poppy grew to over a metre tall. It was lovely to watch its growth, pushing through a crack; it spoke to me of strength, resilience, beauty and growing power. I took many pictures of its beautiful purple flowers and pastel green structure and decided to use these photographs as inspiration to develop a stitched picture. I hung the finished creation on the lounge wall, where it has continued to encourage me. One of the encouragements happens in the depths of winter, when the sun shines through the lounge window at precisely 9am and outlines the exact rectangle of the stitched poppy perfectly in sunlight. It only happens with the low winter sun shining through a certain window that reflects the size of the picture. As it hangs there radiant in the sunshine it continues to speak to me of transformation.

The garden is wonderful to have as a final chapter to this book as it reflects so much of what has been written about inside the retreat house. The many processes that go on in the outside creation can be an informer as well as giving much pleasure. As we enter the garden of this retreat, we will consider how nature can minister to us and be a teacher on our path of life. We can consider the processes we observe in the garden, using it as a place to reflect aspects of our lives and the transformation that is taking place.

As we sit in this garden of the retreat, or walk in nature, we can engage the ways of discovery found throughout our time in the retreat. Sitting and watching, waiting and being still, listening to the sounds and engaging our senses, can bring us into the presence of what the natural world offers. Sir Thomas Browne was an influential writer in the seventeenth century who displayed a deep curiosity towards the natural world. He knew that if you looked hard enough at nature you could see what it meant. 'Nature was there to be read. God had written in nature the meaning of the universe in shorthand, like a secretary. So much was opaque in the world, but those who had eyes to see could see.'[90] Through the natural creation of plants, bugs, animals, sky and landscape, of feeling the wind on our skin and the ground under our feet, we can take the time to let the garden speak to us of our own journey and aspects of God.

In the library there were five big areas mentioned that were difficult to grasp through the logical mind. These five areas of love, death, suffering, God and the notion of infinity can all be observed through the natural world. The garden can show us something of these processes and link to the mystery behind them. St Francis called nature the first book of Scripture. He saw nature as the mirror to the soul, noting that the outer world with its processes and symbolism can speak to us about our

---

90. Quoted in *The Century That Wrote Itself,* a 3-part series for BBC Four, 2013.

truest self.[91] Like my poppy that sprung up in that difficult spot, God reveals through creation ways for our learning for all parts of our daily life, from our sufferings to our celebrations.

To be able to learn from nature we need to slow down and really use our senses, and *Exercise 24* will help with this. Being still and watching the show of nature can be a fascinating exercise. There is so much going on that we will usually miss. Seeing an ant crawling up and down the individual blades of grass, following the blackbird to the nest and seeing her minister to her young, noticing the shapes and colours of all around can take us out of our preoccupations and be a calming influence. Nature is a good listener, we can be drawn to things that speak to us and be a connection for us. What we are drawn to can lead us into the present moment. Rabbi Jonathan Sacks recalled an episode recounted by Iris Murdoch which illustrates this:

> She describes looking out of a window in an anxious and resentful state of mind, oblivious of her surroundings, brooding on some resentment, feeling sorry for herself. Then, suddenly, she sees a hovering kestrel. 'In a moment,' she says, 'everything is altered. The brooding self . . . has disappeared. There is nothing now but kestrel.

---

91. Richard Rohr, *In the Footsteps of Francis: Awakening to Creation* (CD. Center for Action and Contemplation).

> And when I return to thinking of the other matter
> it seems less important.' She calls this 'unselfing',
> and that is what prayer achieves at its best. It opens
> our eyes to the wonder of the world.[92]

The garden has a way of getting us out of our ego selves and connecting us to wonder and God's source of life.

The garden is a place that faces us with the realities of nature. The process of growth, the rhythm of the seasons, the miracle of life and the process of decay and death are just a few of these realities that are highlighted. When we observe nature these realities can connect us to the evolution of the world and our part within that whole. Looking at the process of life and death we can note that our human forms are part of this cycle. I watched an amazing programme about decay that was surprisingly life-giving! There is a whole host of bugs, fungi, moulds, flies and maggots that do so much to decay dead matter and allow the nutrients and gases back into the environment so the world can continue. We are made up of all this decayed matter, as what we eat has in it the nutrients taken from the ground that has been enriched by the decayed matter. We are all made from the same materials and very much connected to the earth. I can see this process as I throw out fruit and vegetable peelings onto the compost heap and somehow it turns into nutritious compost that gets thrown over the soil in

---

92. See http://www.rabbisacks.org/credo-three-resolutions-for-the-new-year/.

my garden to grow vegetables that I then eat. It is such a clever process and I agree with Frances Hodgson Burnett that nature is magic!

We are much less connected to the land in our present age. We buy our food at supermarkets and have many tasks that keep us indoors. It is easy to forget that we are very much part of nature. We can become more open to experience nature by taking time to feel the earth beneath our feet (perhaps taking off our shoes), to experience the different weather conditions, and to feed the birds and grow some plants. This can lead to a sense of belonging as we realise our connection as part of creation.

As we develop a connection to nature we can receive so much blessing if we allow it; it can feed us with beauty, creativity, and learning. As we can see through artists and poets, it can feed our spirit to spill over into other areas of our lives. The sculptor Barbara Hepworth notes that 'In the contemplation of Nature we are perpetually renewed, our sense of mystery and our imagination is kept alive, and rightly understood, it gives us the power to project into a plastic medium some universal or abstract vision of beauty.'[93] Her connection with the garden gave her time to feed her imagination which spilled over through creativity into her work.

---

93. Quoted in 'Hepworth, Dame Barbara' in Ian Chilvers and John Glaves-Smith, *A Dictionary of Modern and Contemporary Art* (Oxford University Press, Oxford Reference Online: http://www.bbc.co.uk/arts/yourpaintings/artists barbara-hepworth/biography).

I found that the garden also fed my imagination and gave me ways to be creative and help with my life. It especially helped me to reflect on my own transformation. It can be difficult to find ways of considering our connection to the path of life and how we are transforming to becoming more whole and healed people. I used my imagination to consider a garden within me and let this reveal to me how my internal journey was flourishing. I was surprised at how an image within me of a garden, that I started to visit as a place of relaxation, took on a development of its own that reflected my needs and informed me how these needs were being met. I didn't have to know the meaning behind the river that formed or the field that appeared, the brambles in a corner that attracted the butterflies, or the time it felt important to build a fire – I just enjoyed its place within me and its reflections. The garden represented an area within that was a place of resting, exploring, dancing and spaciousness that expressed my needs and gave me a visual interpretation of a flavour of my inner journey. It is an image I still relate to; I visited it recently during some atrocious weather that was keeping me awake in the night, and enjoyed the fact that my inner garden was constant, an anchor to me and something that doesn't suffer from the weather! (See *Exercise 25*.)

In this final chapter it is good to consider what we might need to put in place in our lives so that we can connect to the growth and transformation that the path of life offers. The symbolism of the garden and its cultivation offers a creative way of looking at this area. A beautiful garden will need planning and care. Plants need the right environment to grow and space to expand and blossom. For us to connect to the path of life we need to give ourselves space for activities that make us feel connected to our true self; those times when we feel joy, energy, relaxation and a sense of losing time. For me these are blessed times; times that are using my gifts and making me feel lighter inside. The more we continue to explore what is right for us, the more we will be able to flourish in the environment we are in. Plants can flourish in the harshest of conditions if we allow the right seed to be sown; there is always opportunity for light. There might have to be acceptance of our environment and openness to the planting. The garden is not an ordered environment; it flows and weaves, bringing unexpected joys and always surprises.

Discipline needs to be considered to provide the digging and weeding so the seeds that are sown can find space to grow. This might entail finding a routine where different aspects of ourselves – body, mind, spirit and emotions – can be given time. This routine will incorporate the best pace and rhythm for each individual. I have to note my stresses and live a life that is still fairly well paced, to keep my mind and body healthy. This sometimes frustrates me, until I remind myself that this actually gets the best fruit for me. If I travel too fast and don't take the proper breaks then I get tired and my thoughts start to travel down a difficult path. If I don't reflect on the stresses around for me or on things that have had an impact on me, then these will be chuntering along in the background (like something continually running on the computer), making me less alert for the work I do. Our God-given calling keeps us at the point of most health, most fruitfulness and blossoming, and it may entail much sacrifice to get to this point.

The garden is symbolic of the care that is needed in our lives as a whole, so we can grow and fruit. Finding the best disciplines and amount of time taken to tend our garden so that it is given the best chance of transformation requires a delicate balance. There is a middle ground between denial of what is going on in our life and the internal reflections that could get out of hand and become a wallowing within ourselves. There needs to be some momentum as well as pauses for reflection and creativity. The writer of Ecclesiastes speaks of the wisdom of ploughing on with what seems right in life.

> Whoever watches the wind will not plant,
> whoever looks at the clouds will not reap . . .
> Sow your seed in the morning,
> and at evening let not your hands be idle,
> for you do not know which will succeed,
> whether this or that,
> or whether both will do equally well.
>
> *Ecclesiastes 11: 4,6*

There is a sense of risk in this – to continue our work or cultivate our garden anyway, whatever comes along. I take comfort in this as we cannot assess what things we do will make seeds take root, but having a routine in our lives is helpful and can give the right seeds a chance to blossom. There are disciplines we can put in place to aid this movement. Setting times for sitting in the chapel, for reading a book to help our inner journey, and for keeping our body fit to do the work required, for example, can help us to continue on the right path.

I find the three windows which were part of the life of Julian of Norwich to be helpful portholes in viewing the balance and discipline required in my own life. In the fourteenth century Julian, after receiving 16 visions from God, decided that she needed time to decipher and listen to the messages of these visions. She became an anchoress, confined to a room attached to St Julian's church. This room had three windows. One window was open to the church. Here she received her spiritual nourishment from the services carried out in the church, including a regular Eucharist, and from the support of the priests. Another opening was connected to her servant who cared for her physical needs. Julian was able to receive her food and water and pass out her waste. It is thought she may also have had a garden that she could tend through this opening. The last window looked out onto the street. This was a small opening through which Julian could give counsel to people. She would take in any sewing needed so she could earn enough to keep her servant, but she could also give spiritual accompaniment to people, being with them in their troubles, listening and providing wisdom from her cell.[94]

I have looked at my own life through these three openings (see *Exercise 26a*). On a big sheet of paper I have listed under each area what I need to keep in place, or put in place, to maintain the balance in my life. Under the area of spiritual input, I look at what space is needed to be put aside daily, weekly, monthly and yearly to keep a good connection to my true self and the divine. I include what I need to keep in place to explore who I am and my meaning and purpose in life. I assess the books I would like to read and the types of prayer I need to include and what regular activities would be a helpful input. I also look at the relationships that will help with my faith, especially meeting with my spiritual director and the people I pray and worship with. For the second opening I note what is needed to keep my body in the best physical wellbeing, from exercise times to considering what I eat. I note to clean out my mind regularly, so it doesn't get filled with junk and I include the importance of relaxation and rest. Writing my journal and keeping in touch with my creativity is also noted, alongside the people who support me for this

---

94. See Elizabeth Ruth Obbard, *Introducing Julian: Woman of Norwich* (New City, 1995). See also Elizabeth Ruth Obbard, *Through Julian's Windows: growing into wholeness with Julian of Norwich* (Canterbury Press, 2012).

window. The third window is the list of my giving out to others. I note what I need for this window to give the best listening and support and to be able to write in the best way. I look at my giving-out roles of wife, mother, friend, spiritual director, writer and housewife. I note the computer work and regular chores needed in my life. It becomes a document where I can see all three areas and the tweaking and refinement these areas need so there is a better balance.

This is all connected to what I feel my goals and priorities to be in life. I try and have a 'road map' in front of me so these three windows connect to my ultimate aims in life. It is hard deciphering these goals and I try and put aside time to hear the right direction. Once these are put in place, it is much easier to say 'no' to other things that might cloud my vision and to get rid of tasks that might distract. I have a mind that is really interested in all sorts of aspects, so I have to train it to let go of wanting to learn about things that might take up precious time and energy.

Having a routine that incorporates the ploughing and weeding, and having goals and visions to aim for, also assists in the constant battle through life so graphically illustrated in the garden that makes growing plants so difficult. Slugs, weeds, pigeons, hail and drought have to be prepared for and expected – they are part of everyday life. If there is an awareness of the difficulties of life, then they will not constantly shock us. The garden can show us ways of overcoming these hardships, ways that can pleasantly surprise, as my poppy so aptly illustrates.

This routine also brings to our attention the awareness of that growing power that is needed for anything in our garden to flourish. The seed grows within through the 'magic' of energy from our light-filled path. Just as we can watch with awe a poppy that is able to shoot up out of a crack in the pavement, so we can link into this growing power within to notice our own seeds developing into fruit. It can be a recognition of where our seeds are taking root – within the love and centrality of the divine. I like the way that St Julian wrote out her vision, seeing God's work as consistent, with God creating from the beginning of creation through to the end, with the same consistent power: 'Look! I am God. Look, I am in all things. Look, I do all things. Look! My hands never stop working, nor ever will. Look! I guide all things to the end that I planned for them before time began, and I do it with the same power and wisdom and love with which I made them. How can anything be wrong?'[95] Saint Julian saw in her visions that not only can God be seen in nature but that all deeds bear the stamp of God's doing. As we grow, rooted in the divine with its life-giving energy, there will be healing connected to this life, a slow healing that produces beauty and clarity, rather than weeds and stifling.

---

95. Mother Julian of Norwich, *Revelations of Divine Love*, ed. by Halcyon Backhouse and Rhona Pipe (Hodder and Stoughton, 2009), p.26.

The exciting outcome of the preparation and discipline are those times of recognition as to what seeds have taken root. These are only identified when the fruit is seen. The fruit reveals the character of the seed, as well as an explanation of what has been going on within, and so the garden starts to become more familiar. The blossoming of the garden is the fulfilling of our inner development which is not easy to identify but includes an increase in wisdom and transformation of our personalities leading to a revealing of our true self. Paul writes of the fruits of the Spirit which highlight something of this blossoming garden. These fruits include love, joy, peace, patience, kindness, goodness, faithfulness, gentleness and self-control. [96] When I have times of review with my directees, the fruits that might be appearing is one area we consider. It is good to stop to notice any changes in our lives which can be very subtle. There may be positive changes in relationships and in personal qualities, such as different ways of reacting and coping that might be being revealed. Directees sometimes note the ways that they are recognising who they truly are. They might feel they have a voice that connects more to who they are, one that is more assertive and able to express decisions. Noting where joy and peace is appearing in their lives is an important part of this review. One of the changes I have noticed within myself is that I have been drawn to making life simpler. There is a sense of clearing out

96. Galatians 5:22-23.

clutter in my mind and body as well as externally in my house and in how I run my life. (See *Exercise 26b.*)

There are many qualities that can help nurture our garden and keep us linked to its growing power, some of which have already been covered in the other rooms. Being thankful is one of these qualities. Taking time to be still and to be aware of the little things to be thankful for and for the good things that are happening to us can keep the heart open. There are many kindnesses that can come to us that are easily overlooked in the busyness of life. My sister had a period when she kept a journal purely for the good things going on in her life. Each evening she assessed the day and picked out her blessings. It made a big difference to her life. My husband used to commute to London regularly and he had a particular bridge he walked over where he committed the day to God and put on a grateful and positive mindset. Amidst all the hustle and bustle around him, he was singing inside as he started his day.

Thankfulness can work two ways – as well as thanking God and being grateful for the divine's kindnesses we can also receive thankfulness from God for our ministry. Receiving this thanks is something I am still exploring. It was a new idea to me when my spiritual director suggested that I listen out for the times when God is thanking me. I tried to be more aware and listen out for some sort of inner prompting. One day I went out to the garden and noticed that the bird bath was dry. As I was filling it with water, I heard a very clear internal 'Thank you'. I was very moved by this – it felt that this small task was noticed and appreciated by God – a God who cared for even the little sparrows who frequently used the bird bath. Being appreciated for this small task helped me to listen in other areas of my life. I am better now at receiving and letting myself be uplifted by the thanks of others and the recognition from God. Thanksgiving keeps the heart open.

Hope is another important quality needed for our garden to flourish. Viktor Frankl noted in the Auschwitz camp that a sudden loss of hope and courage could have a deadly effect. It lowers the body's resistance against infection and disease. Frankl noticed that the death rate between Christmas and New Year was high, as many of the prisoners had hoped to be home by Christmas. He also noted that the prisoners who had lost faith in their own future were doomed; they lost their spiritual hold and declined very quickly. Hope is connected to finding a meaning in our lives, and Frankl stated that any attempt to restore a man's inner strength in the camp had to connect to showing him some future goal, a reason for living.[97] Hope does not have a direct effect on pain and suffering, but it can keep our minds on a good path and draw us through so we can manage the suffering in a better way. A Mental Health Policy paper has hope as

---

97. See Viktor E. Frankl *Man's Search for Meaning.*

the first component of the process of recovery; finding and maintaining hope, believing in oneself, having a sense of personal control and being optimistic about the future are included in the first step.[98]

Hope linked to meaning, to faith and to our future on a life-giving path is certain. It links into the divine and to the promises and blessings for us. In early Christianity the anchor was the symbol for hope. This is a wonderfully solid symbol with the sense of keeping us tethered and secure in the world's storms. 'Therefore, we who have fled to him for refuge can have great confidence as we hold to the hope that lies before us. This hope is a strong and trustworthy anchor for our souls. It leads us through the curtain into God's inner sanctuary' (Hebrews 6:18-19, New Living Translation).

Hope can be fuelled by memories of times in the past when we have come through difficulties and when good things have happened in our lives. It is good to pause and note these times and celebrate the fruits in our garden. There are stories in the Bible when stones have been used to mark these ways of God. They are often named – as was, for example, the stone that Samuel put up when his people were protected from being captured by the Philistines. Samuel named this stone 'Ebenezer' meaning 'Thus far the Lord has helped us' (1 Samuel 7:12). We can be reminded more of God's enabling if we stop and note and mark out these times,

---

98. Andresen, Oades and Caputi, *Making Recovery a Reality* (2003).

instead of looking out to the next achievement or marching on to try and solve other issues. My journal is a good place to stop and celebrate – perhaps adding a picture or noting something in large writing. Buttons, stones and other pieces from nature can be good visual markers as well. How encouraged we would be if we all had shelves full of markers that noted times of celebration, of answered prayer, of great fruit appearing in our lives and times of enabling.

Our personal garden and its flourishing will be unique for each individual. We need to trust that what we are finding in our garden is right for us. It can be difficult to trust the process of transformation when times are really difficult but that is what faith is all about. We have the resources to tap into the fertile soil within and grow the seeds needed to nourish our life. I heard a story recently from an English vicar who had travelled to Uganda. Whilst he was there, he was very struck by the story of a woman he met whose partner had left her when he had discovered she was HIV positive. She had three children and couldn't afford to put them through school. As her energy decreased she got to the point where she just wanted to die. Each day she awoke with this aim of wanting to die. One Sunday morning the pastor in his sermon told her that God had a plan for her and she had all she needed for that plan. The English vicar would never have told someone so poor that she had all she needed – to him they all had so little. But this pastor did, and told her to be thankful for what she had. She went home and thought about what she had. She realised she had a little plot of land but did not have the energy to do anything with it. So she thought of who she could ask to help her. She got two people from the village to dig over the plot of land and gradually she grew some things and added to her little smallholding, including chickens and a goat. Through the money she made from this plot she was able to send her children to school and gradually she became a woman of respect in her village.

As we travel on our journey and connect to the path of life we become encouraged and find ways to hear the voice of God within. When going through a rough period in my life I read the words Elizabeth said to Mary after she had shared about her pregnancy: 'Blessed is she who has believed that what the Lord has said to her will be accomplished!' (Luke 1:45). I asked myself what the Lord had said to me and looked back at my journal over the last few weeks. Through snippets of things I had read, pictures that I had imaged about my situation and from my writings of what I think God might have said to me, I collected a two-page list of encouragement. It is pages like this in my journal that bring me to my knees in humble thankfulness to a God who guides me through tough times, nurtures my garden and shows me the way to flourish.

I probably won't hear how your journey has been through the rooms and garden of this retreat. As I have travelled through these rooms I have had a sacred and enriching experience and I pray for your experiences you will have had and may continue to savour. *Exercise 27* is a final exercise to help with reviewing this book and your journey through the different rooms. My hope is that you have found something of your true self and the divine that speaks to you. The path of life is enriching and empowering; take your time over connecting to and exploring this path and allow it to change your life. Be expectant and look for the surprises that will come your way.

For Consideration

- What is nature telling me of the transformation process?
- How am I changing as I move through the rooms of this retreat?
- What do I need to put in place to continue my connection to the path of life?

Vanessa's Story

Vanessa had come to a time of review with her spiritual director. They had chosen to spend one of the sessions looking over the last year. She thought it would be good to look back and see what things had changed for her and where she felt in her relationship with God. The main changes she had noticed were in her emotions and ways of reacting. She felt a lot calmer about her life and wasn't getting caught up in panic states like she was before. She realised that this was because she was more aware of what caused these states and her thoughts and feelings about various situations, so she was able to deal with them in a better way. She found that her faith was much more practical. Bringing God into her thoughts and situations really helped her to talk things through and listen to the divine wisdom and guidance. She paused more regularly throughout her day to breathe deeply and link into a calmer, stiller place within.

Working out a way of hearing God's voice through the creative processes had been the most exciting. She now tried having one session a week where she drew out what was going on for her, or used her body to express what it wanted. She then listened to what God was saying to her through these times. It gave her insight into how she was feeling more assured in connecting to herself and the decisions she made in life. There were still a lot of difficult issues around for her but she felt more in control over how to go about dealing with these issues, as well as feeling increasingly supported by her faith. Vanessa had also tried to be more open about her feelings and circumstances to her husband and a close friend. She was now feeling more intimate with her husband and finding better support from her friend.

Something she had recently done was to put a few useful prayer tools in a basket. Vanessa found that it was still difficult to fit in regular prayer times but when she did have some time it was really helpful having a basket to pull out from which she could choose what was right for her in this time. So the Bible and commentary were in this basket, as were her book about the Examen, *Sleeping with Bread*, and another encouraging book, some felt-tips and crayons and the journal that she had started recently. A candle was added to mark the holy ground of her prayer time. Vanessa had also collected her own buttons to use when praying for others, as she found her mind a lot more focused when holding a button chosen to represent the person for whom she was praying. The basket gave an air of excitement to her prayer time, adding to her expectancy of what she might find as she explored her own feelings and listened to God.

Mike's Story

When Mike reviewed his past year he realised that he felt more connected to himself somehow – more at ease in his own company. Whereas before he felt lost and lonely, he now felt he had woken up to himself and was enjoying his new-found self. He was finding out about the things he really enjoyed doing, such as walking in the countryside and creating in wood. Mike had got himself more of a routine now, realising that part of his lostness was that he had no structure to his day. He knew he had to pace himself as his health was still unreliable, so rest was part of his routine. He also put in each day a time of connection to God which included sitting in the garden watching nature, walking in the local woods, or lighting a candle and sitting with that. He didn't really know what went on at these times other than a sense of connection to an important part of himself. Sometimes it gave him thoughts and memories that he found encouraging or that he needed to work through.

These times were supported by the weekly meditation sessions where he was getting to know some people in the group. He had also recently visited the Quakers at their Sunday worship. This was something that interested him, as mostly it was a silent service but occasionally someone would speak out words prompted by the inner Spirit. It was good to hear how God was speaking in other people and to be able to talk to them after the meeting. Mike could still feel that excitement in the way God answered him when he poured out his thoughts onto paper. It was something he continued to practise, especially when something was bothering him or when he needed to make important decisions in his life – writing out his thoughts and then writing on another sheet of paper God's reply.

Mike also found himself supporting some of the causes that were talked about after the Quaker services. He had wanted to give something to the community but had never been sure what to do. Now there were opportunities spoken about at the Quakers to which he could give a bit of his time.

Reading poetry and capturing encouraging phrases was another addition in Mike's life. He wrote relevant snippets in a notebook which was becoming a precious holder of his hopes and dreams. One he had written out to stick on his fridge as he felt he needed reminding of this often.

> What should I say about your tendency
> to doubt your struggle
> or to harmonize your inner and outer life?
> My wish is ever strong that you find enough
> patience within you
> and enough simplicity to have faith.
> May you gain more and more trust in
> what is challenging,
> and confidence in the solitude you bear.
> Let life happen to you.
> Believe me: life is in the right in any case.[99]

---

99. Rainer Maria Rilke, *Letters to a Young Poet* (Merchant Books, 2012), p.67.

Epilogue

This book came about through an idea I had of a therapeutic retreat centre. In my author's note I mention my hope to work at such a centre, and during the writing of this book I explored places in Britain that might offer such facilities. Holy Rood House, Centre for Health and Pastoral Care in Thirsk, North Yorkshire, seemed to incorporate all the rooms in my retreat centre. I am delighted to write that as this book comes to a close I have been given a place to live and work in the community at Holy Rood, along with my husband. It offers space for me to carry out the aspects in this book and so contribute to the life of the community. I am excited and blessed by this opportunity and look forward to noting how my life-giving journey develops.

Details of Holy Rood House are in *Appendix 2.*

Appendix 1

Creative exercises for each room

Personal Room

Exercise 1 – Observing my circumstances

Sit in a quiet place and try to let go of thoughts in your mind. Focus on your breathing, just breathing in and out and get a slow rhythm going. Allow your body to relax. Now imagine that you are climbing a hill or mountain. Try and use your senses to get into the scene – what can you hear, touch and see? Then imagine sitting down and noticing the view. Just accept what you see and observe with interest and without judgement. If it is an upsetting scene, try to sit with it and keep your breathing slow and even. Don't worry if you can't see anything – just sit still and notice whether you get a sense or a glimpse of anything.

Now allow a sense of the divine to come into this scene. This might be in a human form of Jesus or it might be as a spiritual sense, such as the sun shining or feeling the air around you. Use what feels right to you. Notice what happens to your scene. Have a go at voicing something of what you can see and what might be happening. Listen to the perspective of the divine. What is it wanting you to note?

Take time to acknowledge what has happened. Perhaps make a note or a drawing. Has anything connected to your present circumstances?

You may find it takes more than one attempt to get into this scene. You may prefer to think about what it was like for Jesus to go up on a mountainside and pray, and see what develops from your thinking. Once the exercise is practised, it can be a good place to regularly go to assess your situation and talk about it with God. Over the months there may be many changes in the scene. You can also use this exercise to look back – over the other side of the mountain and review something from the past.

Exercise 2 – The Examen

A way of reflection to become aware of the path of life, based on the teachings of St Ignatius.

Take your time with this reflection and start by sitting quietly and letting your body relax. Allow an acknowledgement of a divine presence. Gently guide yourself through the events of the day. Let images and thoughts come into your mind, rather than thinking hard about what might have happened. Take time to notice some of the little things in your day, what might have caught your eye or appealed to your other senses.

Become aware of what caused a reaction within you, of what stirred your emotions. One of St Ignatius' great insights was that God would speak through our deepest feelings and yearnings. Reflect on the feelings you experienced during the day. Boredom? Elation? Frustration? Compassion? Anger? Confidence? Anxiety? What might God be highlighting through these feelings?

Note what has brought you joy, gratitude or peace, or maybe an increase in energy. These will be drawing you to your path of life. They may have come from the people you interacted with, from thoughts or through your senses – from what you have seen, heard, smelt, tasted and felt.

Note where there have been difficulties in your day. Note where there has been a drain in your energy or what has led to unrest or turmoil. These could be highlighting areas for change, or they may be calling to you for more support and nurture. The difficult emotions could be highlighting times when you are being drawn away from the path of life.

Choose one thing that has come up for you in your reflections and let yourself be led into conversation – speaking out your thoughts and listening for divine input. You may like to make some notes.[100]

---

100. This is my version of the Examen. See more at: http://www.ignatianspiritu-ality.com/ignatian-prayer/the-examen/how-can-i-pray/#sthash.LF0x7IGb.dpuf.

The Chapel

Exercise 3 – Ways into stillness

3a – Using a word or an image

Sit quietly and focus on a word that you associate with calm and stillness. It could be Maranatha (meaning 'Come, Lord Jesus') or a word personal to you. Say this word slowly and connect it to your breath. For instance, Mar-a-na-tha could be used to cover one in-breath and one out-breath. Try and stick with the word, not letting thoughts interfere. Alternatively you could use an image to focus on – either one in reality, such as a vase of flowers, or a lighted candle, or one in the imagination, such as a lovely scene you remember. Allow the image to lead you into a sense of peace and stillness.

3b – A breathing exercise

First get yourself comfortable. Then be aware of your breathing: focus on breathing in, then breathing out. Feel the cooler air through your nostrils as you breathe in, and let your in-breath travel right down into your diaphragm. Now feel the warmer air leaving your body. Try and slow down your breaths. So just slowly breathe in and out and concentrate on getting a good slow rhythm going.

Now focus on your body – firstly, let any thoughts that come into your head just drift away – imagine them like clouds sailing off over your head. Then focus on your head – notice any tensions around your eyes and forehead. Let go of any tensions and smooth over any wrinkles. Notice if your teeth are clenched and just relax your mouth. Then focus on your neck and shoulders. This is often an area of tension. Drop your shoulders down and ease the area around your neck. Enjoy the sensation of heaviness around this area. Now focus on the stomach and abdominal area. Feel your breath going right into this area and let go of any tensions around here.

If you have pains anywhere in your body, just breathe deeply into those pains. Try and relax the area around the pain.

Feel what it is like to be relaxed. Be aware of being in the room, in this relaxed state. Listen to any sounds you can hear. Appreciate your mind letting go and connecting with the present. Allow a sense of calm and peace to lead you into stillness. Try and stay with this still state for a few minutes. Go back to concentrating on your breathing and connecting to your senses any time you feel drawn away from this stillness.

3c – Active listening

Use your senses to keep you in the present moment. Try not to let any thoughts dominate this exercise, just keep with your body.

- Touch – note what you can feel.

- Smell – note what scents are around.

- Taste – can you taste anything in the air or is there any flavour in your mouth?

- See – note what you can see before you and around you.

- Hear – listen to the sounds. What can you hear if you listen, and then listen some more?

Allow an opening of your internal ears. Listen in an open and relaxed way, just allowing whatever comes up. Note these things, then let them go and focus again on your senses.

Exercise 4 – A relaxation and meditation exercise to explore the way to our inner sacred space

Focus on your breathing, concentrating on breathing in and breathing out. Try and slow down your breaths to a slow regular rhythm. Go through the body from feet to head, slowly letting each part of your body become heavy and relaxed.

Have a look at your mind – what is buzzing around in there? Try and let go of thoughts. Maybe just think of a colour and hold on to that colour.

Then imagine a path travelling deep within you. It goes into that special inner core of you. This is a sacred space, a holy place. Here it is you are going to meet God. Can you picture a place where you are? Perhaps a scene? Imagine yourself in the divine presence and spend some time in this presence.

You may like to write or draw what you have experienced.

The Kitchen

Exercise 5 – Exploring the heart

5a – Connecting to my gifts

These are a couple of reflections to connect to your gifts. With each reflection take some time to still yourself, maybe connecting to your breath and letting any intrusive thoughts go. As you sit in the quiet, allow any memories to come to you that highlight your gifts. You may like to write them down.

Reflection 1 – connecting to my gifts as a child
Reflect on the gifts you had as a child; what excited you and what did you enjoy? What did you like to play? Are there particular memories that stand out of ways you behaved, moments you were proud of or things you created, that reveal your gifts?

Reflection 2 – further reflections
Allow memories to come up of times of showing your gifts. There might be particular incidents that you are reminded of that show a particular strength, or highlight a positive achievement. Let the little things bubble up – a time you helped someone, a time of joy, a time of feeling fulfilled.

You may struggle to find memories to begin with, but once you start sitting quietly and allowing memories to come to you, you will find more memories gradually come to you over time.

Take these reflections and stand back and view yourself. Try and get a list together of your gifts. These will tell you about yourself and will help you to connect to your purpose in life.

There are good lists of skills and abilities on the following websites to help your exploration: http://examples.yourdictionary.com/examples-of-skills.html
http://jobsearch.about.com/od/skills/fl/Interpersonal-Skills.htm

http://jobsearch.about.com/od/skills/fl/personal-skills-list.htm.

5b – Exploring the heart and its focus

On a large sheet of paper draw a big circle on the bottom left-hand side, leaving some space around this circle. This circle represents your heart. Using colours and words, see what comes up for you as you reflect on your heart which is a store for your hopes, dreams and desires. Try not to think too hard about this, but just start to doodle and add any words and symbols. Reflect on the emotions that have come up for you.

Next draw a path into your heart from above this circle. Reflect on what you do to find a way into your heart. You may want to consider the best ways for you to touch on this area.

Leave some time for this consideration and then add another path coming out of your heart. Explore what this path feels like and where it might be heading. Try not to think logically about this – maybe see it as an image. You might like to note some signs on your path and what they might depict. You might want to add something to your path – maybe some supporting guide posts.

Reflect on this exercise as a whole, letting it help you connect to your hopes and dreams. If nothing has come to you, or if your heart feels inaccessible, then just focus on the path into your heart. Note what time, space, nurture and support you may need in your life to connect to this precious area. Note where the path out of your heart may be heading and consider any changes that might need to be made.

Exercise 6 – Observation with my food and drink

Take some time to reflect on the food and drink that you consume. Reflect on what food and drink mean for you. Ask yourself questions such as: 'Do I often eat food when I don't feel hungry? Do I know the needs of my body, what it is wanting? What is my mood as I go towards my food source? Do I turn to food when I am bored?'

What emotions come to the fore as you reflect? Observe your body and listen.

Be aware of your stomach and guts. Notice what they might be adding to your reflection. If you can, have a conversation with your stomach. Ask it questions and listen to what it says to you.

Be present as you prepare the food or take the food to eat. Use your senses to feel, sniff, taste and look at the food. Notice the sensations of when you feel hungry or thirsty, full or having just eaten. Ask your body what it requires and listen to what it might be saying. Check this out with your heart or in the presence of the divine. Is there another perspective to hear about your food and drink?

The Spacious Room

Exercise 7 – Drawing out the body

This is a creative exercise to explore your body. Take some colours and a large sheet of paper. With your non-dominant hand, draw a rough outline of the body as large as you can on the paper. Still using your non-dominant hand, use different colours to place doodles into the body as your eye and hand lead. Let yourself be led to the colours and shapes to put into your outline. Don't worry about understanding this or thinking about it logically.

When you feel it is completed, look at what you have on the paper. Note the process of doing this: what order did things appear and what feelings did that bring up? As you look at this representation, how does it speak to you? What do you notice that you may not have been aware of before? What would you like to say to this body and what might it say back to you?[101]

One directee who did this exercise found that she drew herself sitting sideways, looking slumped and heavy. There were a lot of jagged lines around her heart. It helped her to reflect on aspects of her life where she is more upright and where her heart is released – examples for her were the love of her family and the Quaker meetings. It encouraged her to do some painting with the

---

101. Adapted from Lucia Capacchione, *The Art of Emotional Healing* (Shambhala Publications, 2006).

non-dominant hand which really 'opened a shutter' for her so she was released further with her creative painting.

Exercise 8 – Connecting and listening to my body

First, get yourself comfortable. Then concentrate on your breathing. Just note how you are breathing: note the rhythm and follow the air going into and out of your body. You may like to breathe more deeply and with a more regular rhythm. To do this, place one hand on your chest (which should move only slightly) and one just below your rib cage (which should rise noticeably) and breathe in slowly through your nose and deeply through to the bottom of your lungs, down into your diaphragm. Pause for a moment and then breathe out slowly and fully through the mouth or nose. As you do this, try and slow your breathing, so that you are breathing in for 4 counts, holding for 2 counts and exhaling for 5 counts.

Now observe your body. Just notice its posture. Feel the floor or the chair supporting you and the ground beneath your feet. Acknowledge any tensions, aches and pains. Breathe into these areas. Imagine your in-breath as breathing in life; as you pause, imagine it connecting to God's Spirit and, as you breathe out, release any tensions or clutter in your body.

Then focus on your heart – listen to its beat. Appreciate all that it does for you. Stress often makes the heart beat faster. If you feel that it is beating too fast, just imagine it slowing down and enjoy being able to relax.

Notice what emotions are around for you. Can you feel them anywhere in your body? Breathe into these areas. Do they remind you of any shapes or colours? You may find a picture comes to mind.

Keep this connection to your body. Use your senses to stay connected. Allow your body to speak to you. Listen to what it is saying. You may find you want a conversation with all or part of your body.

As you take yourself out of this exercise, try and keep in place a connection through your senses as you go about your day. Try and slow up at intervals, noticing what you are touching, smelling and hearing. Savour a particular texture, smell or sound, and pause before you move on.

Exercise 9 – Reflecting on energy

9a – Areas to be aware of my energy

Notice what is happening with your energy in the different areas of life. The following are a few areas but you can add your own.

Observe your physical energy and when the energy is flowing well, or when energy feels low. Notice the best exercise for you, what your body prefers. Note when your body is tired and what you may have done.

Food and drink – observe what your energy is like before and after eating and drinking. Especially note an hour and a half after eating, as this is likely to tell you whether what you have eaten suits your body. Some foods sustain energy and are better for the digestive system, and so keep the energy flowing. Some foods are harder to digest or may be causing problems with the gut. Our energy will deplete with these foods. If you are not sure about this, there are nutritionists who can help with food allergy testing. Drinking enough water can also have a positive effect on our energy levels.

Observing the mind: note how your thoughts may be having an effect on your energy. Observe the thoughts that increase energy, give you good feelings and make you more positive or happier. Note the ones that drag your energy down.

Note your emotions and how they affect your energy. Look for the ones that keep it going and for the ones that drain you. The emotions that have a more negative connotation are not necessarily those that drain your energy. Anger and frustration, for instance, can have a strong energy that could be put to good use.

Notice your energy when connecting to the divine: the times of prayer, of coming into stillness, of worship, of connecting to God.

Observe your everyday activities – which ones drain and which ones boost your energy?

Notice your energy in the rhythms of the day. What time of day is best for your energy? What do you feel like after sleep? Do you get periods of rest and relaxation and, if so, how do they help your energy?

Observe your energy with relationships. Which ones sap your energy and which boost your energy? Notice whether being with people gives you energy or whether it is something you find more draining. Does being on your own boost your energy?

Allow these reflections to tell you more about what is right for you and about your gifts and passions. Notice how they could lead you to a more life-giving path and to being more aware of when you are dragged down.

9b – An energy exercise

The above reflections can be developed in this exercise. This is a quicker way of noting our energy levels and is to be done without thinking too logically.

Take a big sheet of paper and divide it in two. Use colours to draw or write, or use magazines and cut out pictures and words that relate to your energy. On one side, note where your energy flows well. Note activities, relationships, thoughts, emotions, food and prayer that help your energy or input energy into your body. On the other side of the paper, note where you output your energy and what saps your energy.

This exercise can reveal much about your energy and the balance of the input and output of energy in your life. You may need to review this balance, as there may be much more on one side that takes away your energy. This may give you insight into what might need to change in your life, so that there is more input to your energy.

The Creative Room

Exercise 10 – Creative exercises

10a – Using symbols, images and metaphors

Creativity can be engaged as we allow a visual image to connect to our circumstances or feelings. This exercise is a good introduction to link with the listening room which will provide a fuller explanation.

Creative pictures and language help us to sum up what is going on for us. Notice the opportunities that might give rise to connecting to a symbol or image. For example:

When you have feelings you want to explore, see if there is a visual reminder.

When you reflect on your situation, see if an image appears.

When you might need some encouragement, is there a symbol you could connect to?

A metaphor is a figure of speech containing an implied comparison, so a word or phrase is compared to an object or action. You may be surprised at how much you use creative language in your everyday speech; metaphors can crop up regularly, for example, and this can be expanded upon to help explore. 'I don't have a firm place to stand on', 'the world's my oyster', 'I'm feeling blue', 'I need to find the key' are all examples to seize and expand.

When you find a visual representation then allow yourself to explore it. You could:

- Draw it
- Write about it
- Converse with it
- Imagine what it might develop into
- Bring it into God's presence to see what might happen.

One or all of these methods will bring much more understanding to you.

For example, I had a directee who explored the feeling in the pit of her stomach. She said it felt like a brick. This gave her something to work with as she explored that brick and why it might be there. Her options included drawing it out and writing the feelings on the brick and noting what it did to her body. She could also have talked to the brick and imagined what it might say back to her. She could have brought it into the presence of the divine and noticed what might happen to the brick.

10b – Exploring the use of colour

Take some felt-tips, crayons or paints and some large sheets of paper. Let your body relax, perhaps connect to your breath and feel the chair holding you and the ground under your feet. Let your eye attract you to a colour and let your hand lead on the paper. Just see what comes up as you doodle. Keep going, developing the doodles until it feels complete. Sit with your creation and let it speak to you.

You might like to develop this and use colour and paper when thinking about your feelings or your situation. Colour is really good to express our different emotions.

You may find you have an image that you want to express. Let that emerge with the colour, without getting frustrated if it does not look exactly how you imagine. It is more important to have a representation and to note the colours and shapes.

Interpreting your image

You may finish your creation and have some unintelligible markings that are difficult to decipher. To understand your image further it is helpful to note how it all came together – the process: what was happening in your thoughts and feelings when you were drawing? The shapes might remind you of something – is there anything you can see that rings a bell with you? The colours might connect to feelings or adjectives that describe your journey – yellow may be bright and energetic, for example. The more creations you do, the more the colours will mean something to you.

You can also think about where you might find yourself in the picture. There may be a title that comes to mind. There may be one particular part of the image that draws your attention. You could then go on to develop this area further as a later image.

Sitting with your image in the presence of God will bring further insight. You may like to note what difference it would make if a divine presence came into your image. The colours and shapes may change.

I often encourage people to listen for the message that is emerging from their creating and to talk through the process and what has emerged as a conversation with God, or as writing in their journal. Sometimes we don't understand what is before us, as we are not quite ready to receive that information. We will only understand what we are able to receive, so more from the image may speak to us as the months progress.

Exercise 11 – Journal explorings – short creative exercises

11a – Senses

Note one thing that has struck you about each of your senses in the last 24 hours. Perhaps something that has caught your eye or is aesthetically pleasing, a smell you may have been unable to pass by without stopping and considering, or something you have touched. Is there a particular sound you have heard that has connected with you, and what about a taste? What has appalled or appealed to you recently?

Give yourself some lingering time to value your findings.

11b – Writing splurge

Open your journal at a blank page and just start writing. Try not to think before you write – just let the pen lead and write whatever comes to mind. Try not to censor anything. You don't need to write in an orderly way – scribbling all over the place is fine. You might like to give yourself a time or page limit – say 20 minutes or 3 pages; otherwise, write until you feel something has been resolved. This can be cathartic but may also be an unsettling exercise, so give yourself space to sit with what has come out, perhaps holding it in the presence of God.

11c – Using your non-dominant hand

Try using your non-dominant hand to draw or write. Just see what comes up when you give yourself free rein. If you are drawing or painting, start doodling and carry on, noting the process and the feelings it invokes. If you are writing, then maybe develop it into a conversation with yourself. You could ask questions with your dominant hand and answer with your non-dominant hand.

11d – Psalm exploring

The psalms are really good for exploring emotions and situations. Take a psalm and find a few verses that resonate with you. Rewrite them in your own words; it doesn't matter if you go off at a tangent, just let them lead you. You could use colour and shapes instead of words.

11e – Exploring your path of life

Take some time to sit still and connect to your breathing. When it feels right, let an image emerge as you think about your path of life. Don't censor anything, just allow something to emerge. Sit with this image and explore it in your mind. Imagine what you can hear, what you can smell and touch. Look around the image and see what is around. If there is no image, then try and get a sense of what is there – it may be an emotion. See if this emotion has a colour and shape.

Then draw the image or write about it in your journal. Use this to have a conversation with God. Note what you might like to change and what you need to ask God for.

11f – Exploring a snippet of a dream

Dreams can be long and complicated. This exercise involves taking one small part of a dream. Try taking a snapshot of one part.

Write what is happening in the present tense or draw this snapshot (or both). Notice what your feelings are and whether they connect to anything for you in your present circumstances.

Take one of the objects or people in the dream and see what it says to you. To do this, imagine what it would say if it had a voice. Let it speak and perhaps ask it questions and imagine the answer. This will sound a strange thing to do but it can be an exciting way of working. You might find yourself describing an object in your dream and the words you use might be very relevant for you. In my example of the dream where I had a baby trapped between the cot and the wall, I could take the cot and the baby as parts of the dream to explore. As the cot I might say, 'I am the cot that is meant to be a safe space for the baby to sleep in but I have one bar that is restraining; it is pinning the baby to the wall.' I could then be the baby: 'I am the baby, I feel trapped by the neck and can't move. I feel helpless and upset, although I know I will be rescued.'

So you can develop this technique with another object or person and go on to see if there can be a conversation between them. Notice whether what is said is connecting to anything for you now – it might remind you of a past memory or something that has happened recently. With the example of my dream, I could imagine a conversation between the baby and the cot. Baby: 'Why are you pinning me to the wall?' Cot: 'I feel strong and this part of me feels too dominant at times and I don't know how to let go' . . . and so on.

Bringing a sense of the divine into the snippet can also help us understand and work it through. Another perspective may appear; there may be a shift, change or development. In my example, I imagine a light breeze appearing that relaxes the cot's hold and gives hope to the baby.

Don't worry if this all feels too complex. Just sitting with the image of your dream in the quiet can sometimes bring some insight.

The Dining Room and Lounge

Exercise 12 – Thinking over my past

Erikson noted eight stages in the process of development. Take a sheet of paper and note down one side these stages: Infancy (0-2), Early Childhood (2-3), Play Age (3-5), School Age (6-11), Adolescence (12-20), Young Adult, Adulthood and Later Maturity. Sit with the relevant stages for you and see what memories come up. Reflect on the relationships you had at each stage. You might want to take this exercise in parts, reflecting on one stage at a time.

Exercise 13 – Writing a letter to my self (finding different aspects of myself)

Take a sheet of paper and write a letter to your 'self'. This is a letter where you can express who you are and what you feel, and explore aspects of yourself. Try not to think too hard – just start writing and see what happens. What are the words that express who you are? What are the feeling words, what are the character words, what are the moods expressed and what are the adjectives? You might want to just list words that follow 'I am . . . '.

Exercise 14 – Three-legged stool exercise for looking at my identity

Using a large sheet of paper, draw a three-legged stool. Using words and pictures from magazines, see what comes up for you for each leg of the stool. These three areas will be a strengthening and balancing to your identity. The first leg is the relationships in your life – friends, family, community and church. The second leg is your relationship with God, and the third leg is the giving out from your gifts to others.

The following suggestions might help you to review each leg of your stool.

First leg – the relationships in my life

Have a think about the relationships in your life. What do the people close to you tell you about yourself? What do those relationships that irritate or upset you tell you about yourself?

Exercise 14a – Pie chart

You could draw a circle and divide it like a pie chart, placing areas for your various roles and needs in life. Then consider the relationships you have and how they might support those areas. Are there areas of your life that need more support from a relationship? Is there anyone you could consider to encourage a deeper sharing of your journey?

Second leg – my relationship with God

You might like to ponder your earliest memories of a sense of God – maybe a feeling, a connection with nature, an experience of love. You might like to imagine yourself as a child. Were there any relationships that gave you a sense of God – someone who gave you warmth, nurture and love (they may have not had a faith themselves)?

How do I feel the love of God now? What strengthens this leg and what draws me away or weakens this leg?

Third leg – giving out from my gifts

What do I do that uses my gifts and talents? How do I give to community? What is hard for me about this? What draws me to contribute or puts me off contributing?

Exercise 15 – Exploring my relationship with God

How would I describe the divine that I link to, and how would I describe the relationship that I have with that divine?

Jesus had many relationships as recorded in the Bible. You might like to ponder some of these relationships to consider your own relationship with God.

Jesus' first human relationship was with Mary and Joseph. You could put yourself in Jesus' place; feel the love available to you and the interactions that might take place.

Jesus loved little children. You might like to imagine yourself as a small child and see what happens as you meet with Jesus.

There are many relationships Jesus had with adults, such as the woman at the well and his disciples. You might like to explore some of these. With each passage imagine the scene and picture yourself as one of the people in the scene. Let any interactions develop. Allow yourself to hear input from Jesus and what you would reply or do.

What have some of these relationships said to you about your relationship with the divine?

There are many Bible verses that speak of the relationship God would like to have with us, in its many aspects. It is good to collect the ones that speak to you. There is also a good resource at http://www.fathersloveletter.com/text.html.

The Library

Exercise 16 – Observing the mind

Notice at different parts of the day what may be going on in your thoughts. Listen to the thoughts and to what they might be saying. Use a non-judgemental approach to this – stepping back and observing what is going on in your mind. Note these thoughts as well as pictures, memories and tunes. Note what reaction they produce in your body. Are there any tensions and emotions that occur as a result of your thoughts?

Be more aware of your self-talk and what narrative is going on in your mind. Does the narrative remind you of anyone in your past? Is the narrative something that might be said by a loving God? Are there things that you say or thoughts you think that could be part of a script that is going on in your head?

Notice which thoughts draw you to a better way – to feeling happier, more positive, more motivated or loving, more enlightened or valued or more connected to yourself or God. Notice which thoughts pull you away from a better way, making you feel demotivated, unhappy, low in mood, critical of yourself and further away from God.

If you have a critical voice going on in your mind, try and explore it, maybe have a conversation with it. Ask it why it is there and what it needs. What would make your critical voice quieter? Listen for a more nurturing voice within you, one connected to the divine and help it become more dominant.

You could use creative ways to explore these thoughts more; perhaps writing about them in your journal or using descriptive words to try and understand. You could use colour to lead you to an expression of the mind, allowing the pens to lead as you imagine observing your mind.

Allow a sense of the divine to develop your findings. Take your image from the colours when reflecting on the mind into the presence of the divine and see how the colours or image might change.

Talk about your observations from all these thoughts with God and perhaps with a confidential friend.

Exercise 17 – Meditations using the pasture way of thinking

Take a short Bible story or text (the parables are good to start with) and allow it to speak and connect at different levels within. Slowly read a small part of the text a few times and let it sink in. Note if it reminds you of anything in your everyday life. Take out a word that resonates and pause to chew this word over. Use your senses to enrich the experience. What does the word or text make you feel, hear, taste or visualise? Let it lead you in some way; maybe use your body to express something or use colour to make marks on paper. You could use your voice to verbalise something of this experience.

Use other resources: poems, stories and films to find what resonates with you. Stop when you notice something that has caught your imagination, stirred your emotions or given you a feeling of connection. Let the initial word, phrase or image link into your experience and see where they might connect; maybe to something that has happened to you in the week, or a past memory. Allow a sense of the divine into your thoughts. You might like to develop an inner dialogue with God about your experience.

Use your imagination to take you into a scene – one that has stirred you – from a picture, film, poem, novel or the Bible. It doesn't matter if you use the initial scene as a springboard and then find yourself in a completely different setting; just allow something to come up for you. Use your senses to explore the scene. Note what is around you and what you experience during any development of the scene. Bring a divine presence into this scene and see what happens.

The Listening Room

Exercise 18 – Exploring my river

Take some colours and a large sheet of paper and draw your own river. Put your paper with the long side horizontal and draw a rough outline of a river from left to right. On the far left, start to mark out significant periods of your life. Try not to think too hard about this, just mark what comes to mind. You might want to add boulders, whirlpools and tributaries to your river for different parts of your life. Keep going with whatever comes up for you as you think of the main events of your life so far. Add extra paper if needed. Step back and look at your river and notice your feelings and response.

Note what the river is doing now. You might want to highlight this on a separate piece of paper.

You might want to add to your river your sense of God during the different flows of the river, using marks or symbols. Where does the divine enter your river at present?

Is there anything that comes into your mind when you think of the way your river might flow in the coming days and weeks?

Exercise 19 – Exploring the different aspects of myself and God

During our time of being listened to, we may hear ourselves coming up with thoughts or sentences that highlight aspects of our personality. It can be helpful to flesh out some of our aspects so we can connect to them and see whether they assist our path of life or drag us away from our path. Making these highlights into a character or animal helps us to step back and notice them in a different way, so realising their part in our lives. I will give some examples before continuing with the exercise.

Example 1 – describing the character of our inner child. If our playful, energetic, childish nature had a character, what would it look like and how would it react to the different circumstances we are in?

Example 2 – describing the characters of our critical voice and nurturing voice. If our critical voice had flesh and clothing, what would it look like and how would it be? What about our nurturing voice – what would that look like and be like? Could these two characters talk to each other?

Example 3 – describing the character of our inner wisdom or healer. If we find ourselves speaking some wise words or finding ways of healing, is there a sense of a character within who is a wise healer? Would it be a man or woman (or gender neutral) and what would they say through the struggles in your life?

To continue this exercise try and pause when using descriptive words about your personality. This exercise follows on well from the exercise in the Dining Room and Lounge when writing a letter to your self and completing 'I am . . . ' sentences (*Exercise 13*). As you find an aspect of yourself, try and flesh it out. Think of a character – fictional or non-fictional, human or animal – that it reminds you of, or make one up. Draw it or write about it and get to know it. See if it needs adapting or working on; whether it is helping or hindering you.

You could also use two felt-tip colours to ask questions with your dominant hand in one colour, and reply from the character with the non-dominant hand with the other colour. It is surprising and enlightening what can come from these exercises.

Another way of finding the characters within is to see who you relate to in films and books. When I saw the film Song for Marion I could really relate to the introverted husband of Marion who wanted the best for her. Marion had cancer and he resented her doing what she wanted to do in case it made her illness worse. The husband character helped me to explore my own introverted character and what it might be stopping or holding me back from.

It can also be revealing to explore the aspects of God. All our own aspects will be a reflection of aspects of God. When I hear my directees describe something of God I get them to voice what this aspect of God might be like. We may have some characters that come up that are unhelpful images we have of God – for example, they might be too dominant, detracting from the love of God. I think of the directee who felt that God was watching her every move. The character she came up with was a policeman figure who was always watching, making her feel she had to perform well and be careful of what she did and said. She was able to talk to this character as well as hear what Jesus might say to this character. She decided the policeman was an aspect of God that was not helping her in her relationship with God, and we worked through ways of not having this character so dominant in her life.

Exercise 20 – Finding tools to explore my environment

Draw a big rectangle on a sheet of paper. This represents your first-aid box. This is the essential box that you need in your life to cope with your situation. Think about what you need in this box. Either draw or write in what has helped you in the past with difficulties. You could add words of wisdom, include people you find helpful, books that are a comfort or guide as well as helpful strategies.

You might like to add ways of observing yourself and ways of connecting to God that are helpful for you. There may be some things to add that need discipline and routine for looking after yourself.

One directee who did this exercise ended up making her rectangle into a building. Inside this building she drew in a bed for rest, her Bible and a close friend. She added her journal to help her to keep in touch with herself. Outside the house she placed a rubbish bin where unhelpful thoughts could be left, and she also had a garden and swimming pool for relaxation and exercise. On top of the house a cross formed and she realised that this first-aid box represented a holy place where she could meet with God, be listened to and have space for herself.

The Store Cupboard

Exercise 21 – Looking into my cupboard

Take some time to sit still and connect to your breathing. When it feels right, let an image float up of yourself standing in front of a cupboard. This represents an area within you that contains memories and issues that might need to be worked through, as they may be obstacles in your path of life. As you stand and look at the closed door, note your feelings. Note what thoughts come into your mind as you acknowledge this cupboard. What thoughts would be helpful to you as you think about opening the door? Note also your body and the reactions that are going on as you consider this inner space.

Connect again to your breathing, allowing your breath to become calmer and deeper. Feel the ground beneath your feet on the floor. Connect to the solidity, and you might like to connect this to the solid presence of God. You might prefer to imagine the presence of Jesus beside you or a felt presence of the Spirit of God.

From this observer position, imagine what it would be like to open the door of the cupboard. If this is difficult, just think about what you might need to be able to open the door.

If you are able to open the door, have a look from outside the cupboard. Stand firmly in your position and just notice what you might see. Note the reactions going on in your mind, emotions and body, and draw strength from the presence of God with you.

You may want to note your experience or draw what you saw.

Exercise 22 – Handling difficult emotions

22a – Feeling words

The following is a list of feeling words. This list can help in acknowledging some of the feelings that might be around for you at different moments. They are categorised very loosely under headings. You may like to add your own.

Affectionate	Happy	Creative	Interested
appreciated	amused	absorbed	challenged
attracted	buoyant	enthusiastic	curious
close	calm	impulsive	eager
cosy	cheerful	inquisitive	empathic
loving	contented	inspired	engrossed
passionate	excited	intrigued	focused
romantic	exhilarated	involved	immersed
sexy	hopeful	surprised	intent
tender	joyous		involved
warm	relaxed		keen
	serene		purposeful
	thankful		sympathetic

Fearless	Afraid	Angry
bold	anxious	annoyed
brave	apprehensive	bitter
courageous	bewildered	cross
daring	cautious	defensive
determined	dependent	enraged
earnest	desperate	frustrated
enthusiastic	dismayed	furious
independent	fearful	hostile
powerful	fidgety	humiliated
proud	helpless	indignant
reassured	horrified	infuriated
secure	insecure	irate
	nervous	irritated
	overwhelmed	offended
	powerless	resentful
	scared	sulky
	shaky	sullen
	worried	wrathful

Doubtful	Hurt	Sad
confused	abandoned	anguished
distrustful	afflicted	ashamed
evasive	chastened	choked-up
hesitant	cheated	depressed
indecisive	crushed	devastated
mixed-up	defeated	disappointed
perplexed	despairing	disillusioned
questioning	devastated	dreary
sceptical	embarrassed	flat
suspicious	heartbroken	gutted
unbelieving	injured	heavy-hearted
uncertain	isolated	hopeless
wavering	lonely	ill at ease
wishy-washy	neglected	low
	offended	melancholy
	pained	miserable
	suffering	moody
	tormented	out of sorts

Physical sensations

alive	fit	sleepy
awkward	flushed	strong
breathless	hollow	tense
burning	hungry	uptight
chilled	immobilised	weak
cold	nauseated	weary
droopy	refreshed	
empty	rejuvenated	
exhausted	shaky	
fatigued	sick	

Other feeling words

amazed	impulsive	ridiculous
bored	indifferent	relieved
cooperative	jealous	sensitive
delirious	loyal	sincere
distant	pensive	stubborn
envious	phony	
humble	preoccupied	
hypocritical	proud	
impatient	quiet	

22b – Anger therapy

It is good to acknowledge anger within us. Finding an acceptable way for your body to express anger safely – punching pillows, shouting into the wind, kneading bread, flinging a ball against a wall, can all help acknowledge the anger. Having a good vent onto paper and then tearing it up can also be effective in exploring our anger.

Note your energy levels before and after the expression. It can be surprising how much energy can be released when suppressed anger is brought out into the open.

22c – Being aware of the causes of my emotions

Take some time to note the different emotions that you feel. You may like to use the Examen to sit quietly and note these emotions. Our feelings are created by our thoughts. All experiences are processed through our brains, interpreted and given meaning before we feel an emotional response. Note what thoughts may have triggered these emotions. What has happened for you to think these thoughts?

Sit with these findings and note how your thoughts and emotions make you react and behave. Are there any changes you would like to make?

22d – Coping with anxiety and worry

If anxiety is high then taking some time to do some slow breathing can help, perhaps going through the breathing exercise mentioned in the chapel (*Exercise 3b*). Sometimes it helps to have some creative activities available, such as colouring. There are some really good colouring books available for adults. Doing something easy and engaging, such as colouring, knitting, stitching and jigsaws, can help to slow down the high anxiety brain waves. Moving at a slower pace will help slow down your body. Doing this and being mindful of your senses can really help you connect to the present moment where your mind cannot be focused on anything else. See *Exercise 8*.

Music, physical exercise, housework and rhythmical activities such as swimming can all aid with tension and worry.

It can also be helpful to have a time each day to plan and think about decisions and future thoughts. This can be a time when worries can surface, be acknowledged and become part of the decision-making process. Worries outside of this time can be noted to think about in the next day's planning time and not to mess up the present moment.

Using colour and paper to draw our worry can help us recognise the root cause of the anxiety. Use the creative room ideas to express feelings onto paper and to see what they are saying to you.

Exercise 23 – Ways of ministering to my store cupboard issues

23a – The cinema screen

This is a useful technique of watching yourself as though on a cinema screen, making you the observer. It is one I frequently use with directees. There may be something that has happened from which the repercussions are still going around in the mind. There may be an image from the past that is difficult to move out of the head, or a recent image that keeps popping up. Stepping back and observing the screen can help you see the scene and allow a change to occur.

The exercise

Imagine going into an empty cinema. There is the one screen and you can choose where you sit, as near or far back as you like. This screen is there to show you any events or images that you may want to see. Choose one event or image that seems relevant to you now. Keep the event short or stick with one image that comes to mind. Put it up on the screen and notice what is around on the screen. If you are part of the scene then note what your feelings are on the screen. Then note your feelings as you watch what is on the screen. You can stop the action whenever you want. Notice what it is saying to you. Decide what you want to do with what is on the screen. You could bring in a sense of the divine and see what happens. You could talk it through with this divine presence. If it is a particularly unpleasant image, you could make the screen smaller and smaller. You could also decide a different ending to the scene. What would you like to see on the screen?

I have used this technique often. For example, when I have an event replaying in my mind I put it onto the screen and notice my reactions and my feelings. It is easier to associate with them from the observer position. I can then decide what to do with these feelings and whether I need to talk anything through. Being able to change an image can feel very liberating.

23b – Using positive memories to counteract negative memories

If your store cupboard issues involve difficult memories, one way to help with these is to form a collection of positive memories. Thinking of a positive memory first and using the feelings from this when going back to a difficult memory can help with the effect of that difficult memory. So start a collection of really positive memories that give you really good feelings. You might find times as a child when you were held and loved. You may have memories of a wonderful holiday, a beautiful scene or family times. Your positive memories may include proud moments. With each memory take some time to savour it, note your feelings and try and hold onto the good experience.

Now give yourself time to go to a difficult memory. Sit comfortably and do some slow breaths first. Imagine the scene and what you were feeling. You might like to put the scene on the cinema screen from the preceding exercise. Now bring in the feelings and memory from the good experience and sit with them side by side. You can also bring a divine presence into the difficult memory and see what happens. Bring your compassionate and nurturing voice into the difficult memory and hear what you say into it.

The Linn Ministries have written many helpful books to minister to store cupboard issues. They have especially written about healing of memories (for example, in their book *Healing Life's Hurts*);[102] their website is at http://www.linnministries.org/.

Anchoring is a technique in neuro-linguistic programming involving the use of positive images. This is about having an image in our mind which produces a positive reaction in our body. Having a scene from an encouraging experience from our past – maybe something we have achieved or a good holiday we have had – brings with it positive emotions and helps lead our body on the path of life. When I was going through my long illness I used to imagine a picture of myself being

---

102. Dennis Linn & Matthew Linn, *Healing Life's Hurts: Healing Memories through the Five Stages of Forgiveness* (Paulist Press, 1977).

well and strong. We booked a holiday abroad when I was in better health and I have a triumphant picture of myself at the top of a Swiss mountain, arms raised high and fists clenched in celebration, that I can now think of when further challenges come my way.

23c – Noting the presence of God

With all our issues of the store cupboard it is good to stop and consider where God might have been, or where the divine is working now. This entails trying to see the bigger picture in what we are exploring. Sometimes our focus is on one particular image or event from the past. We need to open our internal ears and eyes and try to see what else was around, what other thoughts there might have been. There may be another perspective that will give more insight. Listening for the aspect of the divine and trying to note where this presence might have been felt can enable us to have more understanding of our store cupboard issues.

23d – Re-writing my story

We might have one or more really big obstacles in our store cupboard that have totally affected our lives. It might come from a time that changed the course of our lives to a more difficult route; it might be that we are stuck in our memories with something that happened to us. We may be living in the shadow of these obstacles and they are clouding our vision and stopping us from connecting to the path of life.

The three suggestions above can all help overcome these obstacles. Another creative exercise is to re-write our story. If that obstacle had not been in our path, what might have happened? What would we like to happen now?

This exercise can be really healing. It can help us to connect to a life without our obstacles.

The Garden

Exercise 24 – Connecting to nature

Sit outside – anywhere will do, it doesn't have to be a place of beauty. Allow yourself to quieten, let go of any buzzing thoughts and breathe more deeply. Start connecting to your senses. Observe the scene in front of you; just notice what you are seeing. There may be insects or birds that catch your attention, or buildings, people, shapes and colours. Feel the air around you; notice its temperature, the touch on your skin, the gusts of wind. As you breathe, notice any smells. Feel your connection to the earth. Let it be a stable place under your feet.

Let your focus gradually be drawn to one area and stay with that. Let it speak to you.

Give yourself time to notice what has come from this exercise.

Exercise 25 – Exploring my inner garden

Get yourself into a quiet place and concentrate on your breathing. Try and still your mind. Feel a peace filtering through to you. Now imagine a path; it leads to a garden gate. In your imagination you are going to open this gate and walk through it. It goes into a garden. Stop and look at the garden before you. You may not be able to see much in your imagination but try and develop the scene in your mind. What can you see around you? Can you hear or touch anything? Are there any particular smells around? What are your feelings about this garden? If you can, start walking round your garden. Touch things as you go past. Perhaps see if you can smell some things. Just enjoy developing the picture in your mind.

Note anything that you would like to do in your garden. This is your place to relax, express any emotions or needs, talk to God, build something or dance. Make the most of this space and time.

Bring yourself back into the room. You might like to note down or draw something of what went on for you.

This image is a lovely one to develop. As you go back into the image, you will find things for you to notice and opportunities for you to express something of what is going on for you. It can develop into a special place.

Exercise 26 – Reviewing my life

26a – Balance and discipline:
Julian's three windows

The window to the church – spiritual input

What do I need in place to keep a connection to my true self? What space do I need and what activities help me find my meaning and purpose in life? How am I getting fed and nurtured by my own time with the divine and within a community? I might consider what space is needed to be put aside daily, weekly, monthly and yearly to keep a good connection to my true self and the divine. I could assess the instruction I might need to help me with my spirituality; what books or courses might be helpful? What about the support I have in place that encourages and nurtures my faith? What is happening with my prayer life?

The opening to the servant and the garden – my physical needs

What is needed to keep my body in the best physical wellbeing? I could consider what I eat, my exercise regime, times of relaxation, creativity and play. I might keep an eye on my mind and how to keep that from getting too cluttered. I might consider what is going on in my journal. I could note my relationships and how they might support and encourage my needs.

The window out onto the street – my giving out to others

What do I need to be able to give out from this window? I might review my gifts and look at the different roles that I have in life. I could review the ways that I give out from myself and whether this is the right balance for me. Maybe I could give out in better ways by giving up something. Have I the right support for the different roles I am involved with?

26b – Reviewing the fruit

Can I note any positive changes in my life in the last few months? I might consider my body, my mind and my spirit. Have there been any different ways I have reacted, or is there a relationship that has changed? How would I describe my relationship with God and have there been any changes in this relationship?

If I consider the fruits of the Spirit – love, joy, peace, patience, kindness, goodness, faithfulness, gentleness and self-control – does any one resonate with me?

How am I recognising my true self? – the part of me that feels like the real me? Are there times I can recall when I have done things that have highlighted this special part of me?

How is my connection to the path of life at present? What might be some of the obstacles that stop me from connecting to the path of life?

Exercise 27 – A tour of the retreat – summing up my reactions to this book

Find a quiet time to still yourself and prepare for your thoughts about this book. When you feel still, let your mind wander into the different rooms of this retreat. Imagine yourself in one of the rooms. Pause and look around. Let your mind recall anything about this room. Note your feelings. It is OK to feel angry or annoyed. Just note whatever comes up.

You may like to take each room in turn and note your reactions and anything you want for further thought.

End your tour in the garden and take stock of what has happened to you. You may want to write something down or share your thoughts with someone.

Appendix 2

Useful addresses and websites

Retreats and spiritual direction

There are many places to go for retreat. A good reference book is *The Good Retreat Guide* by Stafford Whiteaker (Hay House, 2010) – and see http://www.thegoodretreatguide.com/.

The Retreat Association is a good resource. They can also help you find a spiritual director.

The Retreat Association
Clare Charity Centre
Wycombe Road
Saunderton
HP14 4BF

email: info@retreats.org.uk
tel: +44 (0)1494 569 056
http://www.retreats.org.uk/findaretreat.html

All retreats will offer a space apart – time out from the bustle of life. They will vary as to how much learning and support they offer. There is one that emphasises many of the rooms in this book. It is Holy Rood House, Centre for Health and Pastoral Care which offers counselling, spiritual direction, art therapy and complementary therapies alongside conference and training facilities in their Centre for the study of Theology and Health.

Holy Rood House
The Centre for Health and Pastoral Care
10 Sowerby Road
Thirsk
N. Yorkshire. YO7 1HX

email: enquiries@holyroodhouse.org.uk
tel: +44 (0)1845 522580
http://www.holyroodhouse.org.uk/

Every Roman Catholic and Anglican diocese should have a person to contact who can guide you to a spiritual director.

The London Centre for Spirituality has a helpful list of spiritual directors and run good courses.
The London Centre for Spirituality
The Church of St Edmund the King
Lombard Street
London. EC3V 9EA

tel: +44 (0)20 7621 1391
http://www.spiritualitycentre.org

Worth Abbey offers retreats and spiritual direction. They run a Personal and Spiritual Growth course over a year that is very creative, leading to a deeper awareness of God, self and others.

Worth Abbey
Paddockhurst Rd
Crawley
West Sussex. RH10 4SB

tel: +44 (0)1342 710310
http://worthabbey.fluencycms.co.uk/The-Open-Cloister

Counselling

British Association for Counselling and Psychotherapy
BACP House
15 St John's Business Park
Lutterworth
Leicestershire. LE17 4HB

tel: +44 (0)1455 883300
http://www.bacp.co.uk

Mental Health

Mind – the Mental Health Charity
http://www.mind.org.uk/

Mind and Soul – Exploring Christianity and Mental
Health
http://www.mindandsoul.info/

Meditation

For more information on meditation and groups:-
The World Community for Christian Meditation
St Mark's
Myddelton Square
London. EC1R 1XX

tel: + 44 (0)20 7833 9615
http://www.wccm.org

Quakers

I have mentioned the Quakers several times in this book. Their website is at www.quaker.org.uk
They have an interesting reference book – *Britain Yearly Meeting Quaker Faith and Practice* – see http://qfp.quaker.org.uk/.

Health and nutrition

I find Patrick Holford's site very helpful –
www.patrickholford.com

On Being

On Being produces a radio show, podcast and newsletters exploring questions at the centre of human life, such as 'What does it mean to be human, and how do we want to live?' They interview a range of interesting people who explore the richness and complexities of life – http://www.onbeing.org